Backtracking
THE WAY OF A NATURALIST

Backtracking

THE WAY OF A
NATURALIST

Ted Levin

Illustrations by
Joan Waltermire

CHELSEA GREEN
PUBLISHING COMPANY
Chelsea, Vermont

Copyright © 1987 by Ted Levin

Illustrations copyright © by Joan Waltermire
All rights reserved
Printed in the United States of America
Second Printing

LIBRARY OF CONGRESS CATALOGING-IN-PUBLICATION DATA
Levin, Ted, 1948-
Backtracking : the way of a naturalist.

    1. Levin, Ted. 2. Natural history--New England.
3. Natural history--United States. 4. Naturalists--United
States--Biography. I. Title.
QH31.L646A3 1987   508.32'4[B]   86-32717
ISBN 0-930031-08-3 (alk. paper)

for Linny

CONTENTS

CONTENTS

FOREWORD

ANYONE WHO HAS BEEN even briefly acquainted with Ted Levin is aware of his exceptional ability to bring the life of nature into his own life and feelings. In our times, that world of the wild has been pushed off to the peripheries and almost lost to sight. He makes it a reality. He has brought his friends and readers closer to the "non-human" people that inhabit the world around us and helped us become humanized by them. The fox and the weasel, the eagle and the marsh hawk, the frog and the salamander become part of our own community. Ted Levin is also a defender, with a serious anger at all those who despoil the land because they refuse a connection with it and who destroy wildlife out of wanton prejudice. He is saying that unless we can be inspired by following the tracks of a fox across the fields into the trees, we will hardly be in a position to know the land we live in. Unless the dawn over the ocean beach is able to lift us out of ourselves, we will live dangerously empty lives.

The reader will find many inviting regions in this book, examples of keen senses, other modes of experience, and ways of life that we are only beginning to appreciate. As an experienced naturalist, Ted Levin is able to coax us toward their acquaintance. He treats all wildlife as occupants of the great house of existence. Within that house, he seems to say, we must learn to be responsible for the occupants and for our own behavior. This is where the universal family resides. In that sense, wasps and cicadas, salamanders and frogs, petrels and marsh hawks, each with an array of extraordinary senses, far from being irrelevant to our lives, become an extension of them and a progression of the human spirit.

Ted Levin is not a "bird watcher" in the usual sense of that term, implying groups of forgivable eccentrics with field glasses around their necks. He is a tireless watcher of all the life that meets his eyes, and he looks out for much that remains unseen. In his world the birth of a snake is an event of prime importance. The ritual courtship of spotted salamanders belongs to a ceremony of earth power and affinity that none of us can escape. He is a humble man, not given to talk a great deal about himself, but he is a dogged investigator and a consistent learner in a way that transcends the self. His commitment to the worlds of life must help all of us who may be aware that we are present at the kingdom but have hardly begun to follow its reaches in ourselves.

JOHN HAY

I

ON CALL

I OPENED THE BATHROOM DOOR, quickly squeezed through, and waited for my eyes to adjust to the dim light. From behind the toilet the fisher screamed, a high, shrill scream that cut to the bone. As I stepped toward her she bolted across the floor, and with her long claws pried open the cabinet door below the sink. She entered it and turned to face me. Her white teeth flashed as she growled, a low, raspy sound like an engine sputtering on a cold morning, that warned me against further advance. I took another step. She backed into a corner and screamed again, holding me at bay with her voice as if I were a total stranger. Getting the fisher out of the bathroom and into the outdoor pen was not going to be an easy task. I paused to gather my thoughts and found myself asking out loud, "How the hell did I get into this?"

I had left Long Island just after the bird migration peaked in late October 1975. It was not an easy departure. As I stood next to my van in front of my parents' home, a flock of grackles and red-winged blackbirds convened in the European sycamores and Norway maples that lined Crest Road. For fifteen minutes the birds cavorted in the tree tops, flying back and forth across the road, noisy and exuberant. Then they left. There was a symmetry to the birds' stopover and my preparations: they were headed south, I was headed north. I was going to study fisher populations in the Monadnock region of southwestern New Hampshire. My work was sponsored by the Audubon Society of New Hampshire and was part of my masters program at Antioch University. Two years later I completed the study, which contributed to a moratorium on fisher trapping in New Hampshire, and began looking for a long-term professional commitment.

The fall of 1977 was a good year for small science museums. President Carter was committed to innovative education, and there was a lot of government money available for a variety of programs. The fledgling Montshire Museum of Science was one of them. A regional center for science education, it was born out of one man's vision and the generosity of Dartmouth College. The college had donated its entire natural history collection to the museum — more than 115,000 items that included mounted birds and mammals; freeze-dried reptiles; amphibians and fish; study skins; bird nests, shells, and pinned insects; and rocks, minerals, and fossils — the oldest college collection in North America. When the museum was barely a year old it had received federal money from CETA for community education. My friend Linny already had a position there, and she encouraged me to apply.

The museum was squeezed into a converted bowling alley on Route 10 just north of Hanover in the heart of west-central New Hampshire and east-central Vermont's Upper Valley. The first thing I encountered upon stepping inside the front entrance was a large European wild boar mounted on a plaster-of-Paris rock and wearing a red felt cap. My second encounter was with Dr. Robert G. Chaffee, the museum's founder and director. He was a thin, tall man with a shock of white hair. I was struck by his wild, bushy eyebrows and the constant flow of cigarette smoke that rose to form an aura around his head. He stared at me intently, raising and lowering a wild eyebrow to punctuate a remark or to question my line of reasoning. He loved to talk, I discovered, and enjoyed listening as well. He seemed to have the patience of a hungry heron.

He spent two hours talking with me, even though I had barged in without an appointment. He told me about his dream for a community science museum that would encompass hands-on educational programs for preschoolers, teenagers, parents, and senior citizens and consist of field trips, lectures, and exhibits that entertained as well as taught. I told him I wanted a full time job with flexible hours and creative opportunities. I said I wanted a sense of place and community, a long-term commitment to a biogeographic region. His eyebrows moved, and with the drawl of a taciturn Vermont farmer he uttered, "A-yup." We talked about pygmy shrews, long-tailed weasels, and lynx, mudpuppies, and timber rattlesnakes. He told me about his stint as a paleontologist at the American Museum of Natural History and more than I can remember about notoungulates, titanotheres and Oligocene fossils. In the end he hired me.

My job description was loose. Very loose. Bob gave me the opportunity to design programs that interested me. So I organized whale-watching trips off Cape Cod; an overnight trip to watch bald eagles along the Mongaup River in New York State; hawk watches from the Gile Mountain Fire Tower across the Connecticut River, from the lookout on Mount Tom in Massachusetts' Holyoke Range, and from Hawk Mountain in Kempton, Pennsylvania. I organized canoe trips on Squam Lake and Lake Umbagog in northern New Hampshire and designed natural history courses that were accredited through New Hampshire's university system. Bob also gave his blessing to an eight-week course Linny and I concocted on the flora and fauna of the Connecticut River Valley. And when we approached him about a ten-day natural history bicycle tour of northern New Hampshire for teenagers, he said yes (even though I didn't own and had never ridden a tenspeed bicycle). Bob was always supportive, no matter what we had in mind. He had faith in the people he hired, and he let them grow in their new positions.

A year later, when our CETA positions had ended, the museum did not have the money to keep either Linny or me on the payroll.

Linny went off to teach ecology at Lebanon High School, and Bob
and I worked out a deal. He allowed me to bill myself as an associate
naturalist with the museum, and with that credential I began my
odyssey as a self-employed naturalist. In return I was on perpetual
call for the museum as a sort of general-practitioner naturalist. For
me it was the perfect relationship.

Bob even found speaking engagements for me. My first assignment
was to discuss loons with the Thetford chapter of the Daughters of
the American Revolution. In exchange I received five dollars and
all the crustless sandwiches I could eat. And when a position opened
to teach geology — a subject I knew almost nothing about — at the
Claremont campus of Nathaniel Hawthorne College, Bob gave me
help in designing the course, reviewed my outlines, and loaned me
rocks, minerals, and fossil specimens. He was there whenever I
needed him, and he made the museum's collections available to me
day and night.

In 1980 Linny and I returned from our honeymoon along the
Manitoba shores of Hudson Bay, filled with images of long days on
the wet tundra, huge polar bears swimming the Churchill River and
lounging on Precambrian rocks, herds of white beluga whales, and
clouds of frenetic shorebirds that paced their lives by the length of
the arctic day. We decided to lead a Montshire trip to the far North.
Without reservation, Bob Chaffee nurtured the plan, making it a
museum function of special importance that received constant pub-
licity. He encouraged us to make this trip different. When we decided
to rent hunting lodges on the bay forty miles from Churchill, hire
a float-plane, local guide, and cook, Bob guided us through all the
preparatory stages. The trip was a success, the magic of the arctic
having touched all sixteen participants. Six months later, when the
museum received a small windfall of money, Linny was rehired.

There was never a dull moment at the Montshire. In 1979 Bob
fielded a phone call about a mountain lion in North Hartland, twenty
miles south of Hanover. Because the last official record for a Vermont lion was nearly a century before, and because the alarmed caller
was an anthropologist from Dartmouth who had studied African
lions, Bob yanked me from a teaching assignment and sent me to

North Hartland. Every afternoon, he said, the big cat left a stand of hardwoods and crossed the back corner of a meadow. The prospect of seeing a mythical eastern mountain lion was awesome, and I promised myself as I drove down the interstate that if the lion was real I'd quit smoking.

When I arrived, three white-tailed deer grazed in the backyard several hundred yards from the porch. The lion was prompt and obliging. It appeared to be as big as the deer and had a long flowing tail. The deer continued to graze, oblivious to the lion. This was very strange, for deer are alert animals, especially when in the presence of a mortal enemy. I left the porch for a closer look. The deer bolted when the door slammed, but the lion, looking smaller all the time, just padded across the meadow. Through a quirk in Vermont topography — the meadow was bisected by a wide swale visually compressing the backyard — the cat on the porch side of the swale appeared to be close to and the same size as the deer on the far side. The lion transformed into a burnt-orange tabby. Bewildered and embarrassed, the anthropologist apologized, and I had to wait four more years to quit smoking.

One afternoon I got a call from a former editor of *Field and Stream*. He told me that seventeen Eskimo curlews had touched down on the edge of his pond. The very existence of the Eskimo curlew has been debated for the past three decades, with definitive sightings being as rare as two-term Democratic presidents. From the editor's telephone description of the shorebirds — plump, grayish birds with long bills that probed the mud with a sewing-machine rhythm — I realized he was sponsoring a gathering of short-billed dowitchers. Then, every year I heard about flocks of golden eagles that were actually turkey vultures, lynx that were bobcats, and rattlesnakes that were harmless milk snakes. One young woman said she'd spotted an owl with a twelve-foot wing span whose grim shadow spread across a state road.

Once I got a series of telephone calls at the museum from a lady in distress. She claimed a big snake three or four feet long terrorized her invalid mother late at night. Until I heard a description, I had assumed the snake was a milk snake. It was brightly colored, maybe phosphorescent, the lady said, and carried a big light like a coal miner's on its head. Every time the snake entered her mother's bedroom, she said, it crawled into the bed and burned the old woman with its bright light. Her mother even had burn scars, the lady insisted. I diplomatically recommended the hospital, not the museum.

The museum was besieged with questions about orphaned and injured wildlife. Animals were brought in without warning, baby raccoons, woodchucks, flying squirrels, and hares. One night a dazed barred owl in a cardboard box was left by the front door. Someone had to be responsible for the creatures, so I applied to the Vermont Department of Fish and Wildlife for a permit to keep native wildlife. Bob Chaffee endorsed my application, and after several months I got the permit.

The most dramatic adoption we made was an orphaned fisher kit that had been found limping on Route 106 in Woodstock by a veterinarian. We moved her into the bathroom, the only room in our log house small enough to confine her and limit her destructive activities. We built her a nest of towels and hid everything we thought was vulnerable. After inspecting the bathroom, the fisher transferred the towels behind the toilet, close to the water pipe where it was dark and cool and semiprivate. There she slept for most of the first afternoon, curled in a tight ball with her long dark tail circled around her head.

Her leg steadily healed, and within a few days she stopped limping. The fisher loved to climb the bathroom's log walls, exploring every nook and cranny. She'd go up and over the cabinet, into the sink, across the counter, and onto the towel rack. To our dismay, she slid open the vanity drawers and heaved out their contents, littering toothpaste, soap and washcloths across the bathroom. Dried flowers neatly tucked in drawers were turned to dust. She smacked the plunger around the bathroom day and night, the dull thud of the handle striking the bathtub sounding over and over as we lay trying to sleep. I wired the cabinet doors closed, emptied the vanity drawers, and removed everything but the shower curtain, the mirror, and the fluorescent light.

As summer ripened and the fisher grew, using the bathroom became more of a challenge. The shower curtain was now shredded and the

mirror above the sink was broken, as was the fluorescent light bulb. Taking a shower was a joke. Water sprayed across the room as the fisher raced from the floor to the ceiling; the wetter she became, the faster she raced. After showering, getting dry became a brisk aerobic exercise as we lurched and danced about the room, the fisher sparring with our feet. Using the toilet was ludicrous. She'd sneak up on us from behind the water pipe, nip an exposed Achilles tendon, then slip away to safety. Dastardly, ungracious attacks. Fed up, Linny resorted to wearing winter boots in the bathroom and showering outside with the garden hose. Finally, I promised Linny I would get the fisher out of the house and into the outdoor pen we'd built for her. The next morning, before Linny drove off to the museum, I assured her the fisher would be out when she returned.

After six hours I had exhausted all conventional methods of capture. The door of the Hav-a-hart trap was jammed, the roof of the carrying case torn off, and the fisher and I were both still in the bathroom. And both of us by now were deeply disturbed. In desperation I baited a garbage pail with dog food and attempted to usher her in with a plunger, holding the lid ready in my other hand to seal off her escape. Unfortunately she never allowed more than three-fourths of her body to enter the pail; one hind leg always gripped the rim in such a way that she sprang out the moment the lid was brought into action. Valiantly wielding my plunger and lid, I became St. George to her minuscule fierce dragon. When Linny returned she found me sitting on the edge of the bathtub with a blanket around my shoulders, wearing a pair of long stove gloves and gripping the lid and plunger. I was staring maniacally at the fisher, who clung to the log wall and was wedged against the ceiling.

Exhausted and reduced to little more than a village idiot, I had clearly lost my perspective on the task and was ready to concede the bathroom to the fisher. Linny took charge and ordered me out of the bathroom until I calmed down. We broke for dinner, and when we finished, Linny claimed that the animal's shrill, horrifying scream was simply a bluff, and that she would reach in the cabinet — the fisher's preferred retreat — with gloved hands, cast all fear asunder, and yank her out. But when we opened the cabinet, the hairs on the fisher's back bristled. She hissed and growled, then screamed. Linny froze, impaled by the wild sound. We backed off.

We decided instead to chase the fisher into the broken Hav-a-hart trap, which now had to be operated manually. We would cut off all avenues of escape from the cabinet, place the trap in front of one of the doors, and open the door just enough so the fisher, if given to flee, would bolt from the cabinet directly into the trap. It was a plan hatched in despair, but it worked.

Linny opened the cabinet. The fisher, her lips curled and teeth bared, split the momentary silence with a scream and sprang into the Hav-a-hart. I released the rod out of self-preservation and the door slammed behind her.

Backtracking is a habit of mine. When I come upon an animal's tracks in the woods I often find myself moving back against the animal's direction to trace where it started from. In writing this narrative about my encounters with wildlife, I found myself possessed of the same habit. I was drawn back instinctively over my own tracks, back to my boyhood in Long Island, to the ocean, and to the experiences that formed me and led me to where I am today. It seems that's how I like to travel. The old familar terrain, it turns out, is in a state of flux — just as I am — so that, with the passage of years, each return trip brings new surprises.

2

WANTAGH:
MANDELBAUM'S BUSHES AND BEYOND

THE JUNIPERS AND THORN BUSHES along the side of
Mandelbaum's house are now so big that their branches touch, screen-
ing the lawn from the sun and forming an impenetrable barrier, a
great prickly wall. I used to be able to dive over those junipers and
run figure eights between them to avoid being caught in freeze tag,
but when we played stickball, they ate our bright new Spauldings.
Every summer I collected bumblebees and honeybees and bald-faced
hornets from the little white flowers of the thorn bushes. And in
September praying mantises were there, cementing Styrofoamlike
egg cases around the twigs.

When I was in the fifth grade my mother found a mantis egg case
in our side yard, close to Mandelbaum's bushes. She had no idea
what it was; neither did I. I brought the egg case — a flattened mass
of hard, brown foam that encircled a twig — to school, put it in
my desk, and without the slightest bit of speculation forgot about
it. Several months later my desk was a nursery for young mantises,
and Mr. Fazio, a rather mild-mannered sort, encountered his first

great crisis of the spring: no one wanted to stay seated. The girls were afraid their desks were infested, and the boys, with all the bravado the ten-year-olds could muster, captured the young mantids and wore them like badges.

Once the little mantids were rounded up and released from the second-story window, the class settled down, and I publicly dedicated myself to mantid natural history. It was then that I discovered that Mandelbaum's bushes were a mantid haven. All those flowers attracted lots of insect pollinators, which in turn attracted predatory insects like the praying mantis. There were dozens of adult mantises around Mandelbaum's, maybe a whole gene pool evolving in isolation from the rest of the neighborhood. I called them the Mandelbaum mantids, *Mantis religiosa mandelbaumensis*, a subspecies that remains unrecognized in most entomological circles.

To my surprise my father had some light to shed on mantids. He claimed — and his testimony was supported by several members of the Wantagh Jewish Center Bridge Club — that the praying mantises were protected by law, and that killing one was tantamount to shooting a deer out of season. A fifty-dollar fine, he said, would be levied against any offender, child or adult. He stated his case emphatically and the bridge players agreed, but something was amiss. Who, I wondered, would ever know the fate of these oriental insects? I had never seen a fish and wildlife officer drive down Crest Road, and the few police cruisers that periodically zipped past our house were always going too fast to spot mantises. Max Mandelbaum was certainly not an undercover Mantid Warden. He never seemed to notice the fragments of nature that hopped or crawled or flew from one shady corner of his property to another. Max and Rose were quite tolerant, however, of my interest in their bushes and my use of their backyard as a shortcut home.

One September morning as I was inspecting the thorn bushes, I found a robust, brown-green praying mantis dining on a smaller, browner mantis. This macabre sight was, according to some authorities, the consummation of mantis mating. The big mantis was the female. Since the adults die with the frost, this would be her largest and last meal before she laid her eggs. His body would nourish the eggs as his sperm had fertilized them, the ultimate in insect altruism and Darwinian selection; once the male has passed his DNA along to the next generation, his body becomes an expendable source of protein.

There is another twist to this bizarre story of connubial bliss, one I'm sure neither Mandelbaum, the bridge club, nor my father ever suspected. According to one biologist the male mantis is a better lover after his mate has relieved him of his head and upper thorax. He gave a neurological explanation for the success of a headless mantis. A ganglion in the head inhibits the copulatory movements of a male mantis by overriding the activity of the two ganglia associated with mating. The thoracic ganglion, located in front of the abdomen, is responsible for the insect's body English. The last abdominal ganglion controls the mating urge. After the female eats her spouse's head, he, like a veteran of Freudian analysis, loses all sexual inhibitions and becomes, for those last glorious moments of life, a virtual mating machine. If Mandelbaum only knew what dark business lurked in his bushes.

Those juniper and thorn bushes, which formed a great green "C" from the corner of Crest Road to the end of my parents' common property line, were also a gathering place for Fowler's toads. For them it was the perfect retreat from the Long Island sun. At night the toads fanned out to hunt insects beneath the lights of the street and porches and hopped across our front lawn to the side of the house. Every summer a few of Mandelbaum's wayfaring toads, small ones as well as big ones, would leap over the aluminum lip of our window wells and become trapped. For the toads, confinement was not bad. There were plenty of pillbugs and harvestmen, a good mulch of leaves, and lots of shade and moisture, and the soil was loose for digging. But there was no escape. Except for missing the breeding season and being transferred to sprinkling cans and jars for public display, my toads prospered, growing fat and indolent, consigned as they were to life in a window well.

The Fowler's toads had their roots beyond Mandelbaum's bushes, around the block and across the street in a sump on Maxwell Drive. Called a "suburban water recharge basin" by city planners, the sump

collected run-off from the web of storm sewers that ran beneath our streets. It was separated from the rest of the neighborhood by a chain-link fence and formed a centerpiece that attracted neighborhood toads. There were other, larger, sumps around, but this sump was the closest to Crest Road. Every June, toads gathered in the weedy shallows, filling the nights with their loud nasal bleats. *W-a-a-h, w-a-a-h*. When the wind blew onshore their voices seeped into my bedroom. Other animals visited the sump, too. There were garter snakes and ribbon snakes, green frogs and dragonflies. Once in a while a raccoon left the greenbelt on Woodbine Avenue to forage in the sump, and I once saw an opossum down there. Rumors circulated among the more adventurous boys that a long, thin mammal, perhaps a long-tailed weasel or a mink, traveled through the storm sewers from one sump to the next.

But it was the Fowler's toads that formed my umbilical connection to natural history and its complete and dependable cycle. From egg to tadpole to toadlet, I traced the toads' lives. And from the sump to Mandelbaum's bushes to my window wells, I watched them grow. The tadpoles' mid-July exodus from the water was a suburban spectacle. They moved by the thousands, toads so tiny three fitted on a dime. I had to be careful where I placed my feet. Toadlets closest to the water had nubbin tails, those farther away were tailless. Each summer the gray-tan toadlets assembled in the wet grasses by the sump and grew fat on a steady diet of midges and aphids. By the time they hopped to Mandelbaum's bushes they had swelled to the size of a quarter. Had I run a transect from the bushes to the sump, measuring toads along the route, I would have found a gradual transition in size inversely correlated with the distance from the sump: the smallest toads were always closest to the water. Fowler's toads were also my third-grade currency: I traded them like baseball cards. Mike O'Rourke gave up a DeKay's snake for three, a transaction I'm still proud of. Ian Jefferies was always ready to part with a praying mantis, even-up. A red-backed salamander was worth two toads, a newt three.

If Crest Road was a river, Mandelbaum's property was its delta, a rich biologic zone where the road flowed into Martin Drive just north of the Maxwell Drive sump. Martin curved toward the north, draining Pleasant Drive and Campbell Road before emptying into Jerusalem Avenue, the Mississippi of the neighborhood. Jerusalem Avenue was so big that Nassau County ran a bus line from its headwaters in urban Hempstead all the way into the hinterlands of North Massapequa. It was a major boundary in my life. Kids on my side of the avenue attended Wantagh High School, those on the other side, MacArthur High. For all practical purposes, the area across Jerusalem Avenue was Levittown — calling it North Wantagh, as the post office did, just confused things.

Every morning before school I walked my recalcitrant beagle, Corky, up Crest Road to the vacant lot on the corner of Jerusalem Avenue where Crest and Maxwell flowed together. Here, goldenrods and milkweed grew to fruition, grasshoppers and crickets filled the late summer with their stridulating chorus, and monarchs paused on their way to Mexico. There were orb weavers with large dewy webs, brown slimy slugs, and ten million pillbugs. Beneath the discarded billboards and tires that mysteriously gathered in the lot, I caught garter snakes, sometimes thin brown DeKay's snakes, and baby Fowler's toads.

Across from the vacant lot, on the other side of Jerusalem Avenue, stood the Wayside Bar and Grill, a dangerous place. Never was I inside, but behind that loud brick building — which looked more like a gas station than a saloon — was the largest sump in my extended neighborhood, the toad capitol of North Wantagh. In July, after the tadpoles had completed their rapid metamorphoses, Jerusalem Avenue became a scene of carnage. Tiny toads, innumerable tiny toads, were pulverized so flat by the traffic that they peeled off the pavement like cartoon characters crushed by a steam roller.

Next to the vacant lot was an abandoned one-room shack. Inside was decrepit furniture, newspapers from the forties and the oldest collection of *Playboy* magazines I have ever seen. The girls were still half-dressed. Beneath the shack lived chipmunks and white-footed mice, and on the outside walls fence lizards sunned themselves. When I was in the fourth grade I caught a big beautiful box turtle on the lot side of the shack. I kept the turtle for two years in the well below the kitchen window, feeding him lettuce, fruit, and chopped meat. I brought him to school (he was a regular guest at Friday's show-and-tell period), to Cub Scout meetings, and to picnics. For recreation, the turtle — under my strictest supervision — plodded about the front lawn and swam in the wading pool. In autumn he hibernated with the toads beneath the soil and leaves that collected in the window well, and in spring I waited with bated breath for him to awaken. The box turtle remained a treasured member of my menagerie until that ill-fated day when construction workers paved over a part of our backyard, entombing him in cement.

The fate of the garter snake I caught beneath a rotting plank in front of the shack was more pleasant. When I grabbed Queenie, she released a foul-smelling fluid from her cloaca and bit my finger. After unhinging her jaws she began, with a little wave of muscular contraction, to walk her mouth up my finger millimeter by millimeter. Most of my pet garter snakes I released each autumn, but I kept Queenie for three years. She was special. When I had found her, she was pregnant.

Two weeks after she took up residence in my bedroom, Queenie gave birth to seventeen wriggling snakelets. I had told no one the garter snake was expecting. If word had gotten out, Queenie would have been back by the shack in the vacant lot. According to my parents one snake was tolerable, two was pushing my luck, and three was a felony. I wasn't home when the birthing began. My mother was. Grasping the importance of the situation, she telephoned me at a friend's house. Within minutes a congregation of kids pressed against the sides of the terrarium and watched as Queenie dilated and contracted her muscles, sending a series of wavelike motions down the sides of her body. Peristalsis. She continued until the distended cloaca three-quarters of the way down her body parted and a gelatinous envelope containing one folded baby snake slid out.

After the third or fourth birth the novelty wore off and my friends resumed their game of Wiffle ball. I stayed tuned in all afternoon until Queenie was through — for me it was the best show around. Seventeen snakelets, each six to eight inches long, squirmed about the terrarium, nosing in and out of cardboard tubes. The more the snakes moved the more they rubbed against the rocks, loosening the skin around their lips which split and peeled back like husked corn. Transparent sheets revealing each articulated scale hung from their necks. When they stopped shedding, relief maps of their external topography littered the terrarium. Even the pinpoint openings of the nostrils and the buttonlike coverings of the eyes were there: the snakes had literally crawled out of their skins.

I kept one snakelet, Junior, and released the rest in the shade of Mandelbaum's bushes. Junior lived in a small terrarium, a living diorama which I periodically redesigned to resemble a weedy river, a shady woods, and a vacant lot. My friends thought it odd that I devoted so much time to a snake, meticulously repairing its exhibit, but whenever I proclaimed it was feeding time at the Crest Road Serpentarium they gathered for the show. Before the leaves fell, I sent Junior to the Mandelbaums' to find a suitable spot below the frost line to pass the winter — in the recesses of an anthill or beneath a blanket of peat moss. When Queenie died three years later, I buried her in a shoe box in the backyard.

Two blocks south of the vacant lot, down Seaman's Neck Road, is Woodbine Avenue. Woodbine was the perfect name, for behind the synagogue on the southeast corner was the beginning of a great greenbelt. Hemmed between Seaman's Neck Road on the east and Wagner Street on the west, the belt extended from the synagogue's parking lot south for more than a mile to the edge of Park Street. A small brook ran through its woods. Until I went off to summer camp in central New Hampshire at the age of ten, the greenbelt was the wildest place I knew, a frontier. As a seven-year-old I explored it on an imaginary horse. Later I broke trail there as a cavalry scout, and my friends and I played at being Davy Crockett, Maverick, and the Lone Ranger. Later still we choked on my father's cigarettes there.

When I was three or four years old my father took me for a walk through those woods to the edge of a farm pond where dairy cattle came for an afternoon drink. I remember the big red dairy barn across Seaman's Neck Road, the old white farmhouse, and the farmer leading his herd across the street. The cows were the first I had ever seen, and my image of them crowding around the pond has crystallized.

They were my elephants, rhinos, and wildebeests, and the pond a watering hole on the African veldt. Then in 1952 the farmer sold his land. Suburbs slid across his pasture. A high school went up where the red barn stood. No more cows. The pond reverted to a meadow, cut by the brook. The farmhouse still stands, though, tall and white like a tombstone set between tract houses, a mute testimony to the last working dairy farm in the area. It now seems as out of place as my memory of the cows.

When I was a Boy Scout, I took to the greenbelt to earn my nature merit badge. It was then that I began to recognize some trees: black cherry and red maple, American beech and sweet gum, black oak, tulip, sassafras, and white pine. When the synagogue expanded its parking lot my father rescued a spicebush and a sapling white pine and transplanted them to our yard. Both flourished. Every spring the spicebush sent out fragrant yellow blossoms, and in autumn — more than a decade after my father had planted it — the pine dropped its first cone. My parents lost the spicebush to a hurricane seven years ago, but the pine still drops cones, some from as high as thirty feet.

In the greenbelt I saw my first black racer, caught my first ribbon snake, and followed the muddy Lilliputian prints of raccoons downstream to their dens in hollow trees. Where the brook drained into a storm sewer on the east side of the synagogue, I caught green frogs. Not far from there some boys killed a milk snake. One October afternoon in the midfifties, while the rabbi delivered a particularly long Yom Kippur sermon, I could sit still no longer. I left the service wearing my sports jacket, tie, and yarmulke to catch green frogs. Instead of frogs I found a gathering of older boys, equally bored with the sermon, who claimed they had just killed a deadly coral snake and that the snake could strike even though it was dead. I knew Long Island was too far north for coral snakes, so I poked my head through the crowd for a look. The battered snake was about two feet long, smooth-scaled and tan, with black-bordered brown blotches on top and a black-and-white checkerboard belly. When I timidly told them they had bludgeoned an inoffensive milk snake, a relic of pastoral Long Island, they scoffed at me. But I never saw another milk snake in Wantagh.

In the greenbelt I developed the habit of turning over rotting logs. Under almost every log lived a skinny, wiggling salamander. Red-backed salamanders, I discovered many years later, are an indicator species of beech-maple woodlands and are abundant wherever the deciduous trees are tall and the soil undisturbed. On Long Island they were favored by development. Spotted and marbled salamanders, which depend on temporary woodland pools for their tadpole nurseries, quickly disappeared in the presence of bulldozers and asphalt. Red-backs, however, hang their eggs from gelatinous stalks in the cavities of rotten wood. There is no free-swimming tadpole stage; metamorphosis occurs within the egg. When the eggs hatch, little salamanders — miniature replicas of their parents — wiggle out. Like Fowler's toads with their rapid metamorphoses, and garter snakes with their catholic feeding habits, red-backed salamanders were pre-adapted to suburban sprawl (as long as the greenbelt remained unmanicured).

In more extensive beech-maple woods, red-backed salamanders are pillars of the forest community. While at the Hubbard Brook Experimental Station in the White Mountain National Forest I learned they are the most abundant vertebrate, the most efficient converters of energy in the forest food chain. Red-backs far outnumber rodents, shrews, and songbirds, and because salamanders are cold-blooded and lazy, they waste little fuel keeping their stoves stoked. By virtue of their abundance and cold-bloodedness red-backed salamanders collectively store great quantities of energy, transforming more of what they eat to biomass — muscle, sperm and egg — than hot-blooded birds and mammals. They are in effect woodland batteries, storing cheap, efficient energy for the next trophic level, the salamander eaters. All this, of course, meant little to a fourth-grader. In the greenbelt red-backed salamanders were just another wild quarry. Subterranean and nocturnal, they did not make engaging pets. And I learned, after keeping one in a jar on the dashboard of my mother's car, that prolonged exposure to the sun turns a salamander into a lifeless twist of leather.

Hunting for red-backed salamanders was also fun because I never knew what color phase I would catch. Some were gray, more were red. The red form is a classic example of the Batesian theory of mimicry. The color, selected through unnumbered generations to resemble the toxic red-eft stage of the red-spotted newt, protects the salamanders. When potential predators learn that efts taste bad, they also pass up red-backs. The greenbelt supplied the neighborhood with feeder birds, too. Every winter morning downy and hairy woodpeckers, blue jays, and sometimes chickadees fanned out from the woods to breakfast in the suburbs. By dusk the birds returned to roost. Common grackles, big, noisy, and iridescent, lived in the pines. When they paused in the front yard to grub for worms, light ran through their feathers like a fire, manufacturing greens and purples and blues. White-breasted nuthatches wandered up and down the tree trunks, and in spring, gaily colored migratory birds came to the woods like pilgrims: tanagers and orioles, warblers by the dozens.

Mammals were another matter. For red fox and white-tailed deer, the greenbelt was too small. Cottontails and gray squirrels were common, though. Every evening rabbits left the woods to graze on the manicured lawns of Woodbine Avenue, and once in a great while one hopped all the way over to Crest Road, about five blocks away, taking up residence in Mandelbaum's bushes and sometimes beneath the weeping hemlock in my parents' backyard. Squirrels spread from the black oaks in the greenbelt north to the edge of Jerusalem Avenue, building their nests in attics and tool sheds. I saw my first opossum on Woodbine Avenue. It was big, gray, and slow as it ambled through the beam of my mother's car's headlights. When raccoons reached the sump on Maxwell Drive it was because they roamed away from the greenbelt. A friend of a friend shot a long-tailed weasel at the edge of a new subdivision not far from where the old red barn stood.

Weasels had better luck in the marsh grasses along the edge of Great South Bay, and in the dunes across the bay at Jones Beach State Park. A friend who was fishing from a wooden dock in the park watched a weasel chase down and kill a large rat. Both animals, he told me, ran around the horseshoe-shaped dock, brushing past his bait bucket, before the weasel overtook the rat and tumbled down the steps locked in a death grip. Between my junior and senior years in high school, while hiking in the pine barrens of eastern Long Island, I came upon a pair of courting long-tailed weasels. Sleek and brown, they raced back and forth across the trail, stopped, looked me over while standing erect, then disappeared into the blueberry thickets.

Whenever I wanted to learn more about our local wildlife, my mother drove me to the Long Island Natural History Museum on the south side of Sunrise Highway, just east of the Seaford-Massapequa line. The museum was in a converted white farmhouse three stories tall surrounded by a hundred or so acres of second-growth woods. A meandering stream cut through the preserve, passed under Merrick Road, and eventually emptied into Great South Bay. Everyone called the museum and its greenbelt "Tackapusha." The name was borrowed from the Massapequa tribe — of which Wantagh was a chief — of the Algonquin Indians. I never knew what the word Tackapusha meant, but to me the land and building were blessed.

Downstairs in the farmhouse was a collection of native wildlife — a hodgepodge of mounted birds and mammals that looked as if they had been prepared in the dark — a few live specimens, a library, and an old man, the curator. He fed the northern water snakes, ribbon snakes, Fowler's toads, and a crippled red-tailed hawk, dusted the mounts, and dispensed information. He told me that Long Island was no longer a haven for mammal predators, that the wolf, mountain lion, and black bear were gone before the American Revolution and the bobcat by the middle of the nineteenth century. Of those species that survived into the twentieth century, I learned the otter and gray fox were so rare that their existence on Long Island is questioned, and the short-tailed weasel is known only from two study skins. The striped skunk is restricted to the remote portions of the sandy oak-pine barrens and the mink to the cleaner, less accessible marshes. Red fox and long-tailed weasel, he said, survive in the larger state parks along the beaches, on the north shore where there are still some big estates, and out east on the potato farms and pine barrens. Only the raccoon is common.

The old man remembered. He remembered when Wantagh was green with woods and farms, a rural hamlet far removed from the influences of the City. He enjoyed Fowler's toads but remembered when the frog choruses were more diverse and kept pace with the changing seasons. And when mink, kingfishers, and herons waited at the water's edge for the frogs to march. He still collected toads each spring from the small ponds behind the museum. Once he lead another boy and me to a pond choked with cattails and phragmites, filled with black toad tadpoles and tiny sunfish. We seined the shoreline with aquarium nets, scooping dozens of tadpoles — some with legs, some without — for a museum display. He had the best job on Long Island.

3

IN A VERNAL POOL

SOMETIMES I FORCE SPRING. I cut willow sprigs and a stout twig each from a red maple, silver maple, and aspen. I place the naked bouquet in a vase on a windowsill that faces south. Within a week the willow buds swell, and a week later the forerunners of male flowers, the soft gray pussy willows emerge. A few days after that both maples and the aspen leaf out.

A series of springs known locally as the "Indian Springs" (after the Abenaki who once used the clear water to fill their gourds and birch vessels) surfaces by our neighbors' driveway. It creeps across their land, flows through a ribbon of maple and pine, goes under a stonewall, and moves onto the south side of our property. Our log house sits on a small knoll and faces west, with a view beyond the garden to where the land flattens and the water spreads. From the porch I can see the heads of cattails, the thin red lines of red osier dogwood, a tangle of alder and willow, and the water as it trickles around the marsh plants and into a small man-made peat pond by the corner of the driveway. My neighbors once dug peat and collected black spruce cones, some more than a thousand years old, from the pond, for the entire wetland was the mantle of an old woodland bog. Everywhere the land is spongy. After snow-melt and spring rain the pond fills and an intermittent brook carries the water out through a culvert beneath Webster Road downhill to the Ottauquechee River. Our portion of the wetland, flanked by willows and clogged with rushes and cattails, stretches for less than an eighth of a mile and is shaped like the handle of a telephone. From early April to mid-August, frogs are constantly on the line.

On the other side of our driveway, just behind the mailbox lies a small vernal pool — literally, a "spring pool" — which fills with snow melt and rain. By midsummer the pool is dry. Wood frogs collect there just after the pussy willows burst through their bud scales, and their voices, together with those of the peepers across the driveway, give our front yard a stereophonic aspect. Neither the bass of the wood frogs nor the treble of the peepers is adjustable, so I move around the yard until I face in the right direction, and find a balance of sound. Then I listen to that nascent swell of life, that maddening urgency — the most often heard and least seen rite of spring. Eventually my skin tightens, and I am compelled to go to the water to watch the aqueous celebration. There is nothing else like it.

Our wetland is a legacy of the Ice Age, which bequeathed thousands of other wetlands throughout the Connecticut River Valley. By April, after the first warm rain has tugged at the frozen ground, the pond, marsh, and woodland pools come to life as amphibians return to breed. I mark the progress of spring by the succession of frogs and salamanders that enter the water to court and reproduce. The first of these, the wood frog, calls from open water before the ice is gone. By mid-April spotted salamanders and spring peepers show up. When apple blossoms scent the orchard American toads begin to croon, followed in late May by gray treefrogs and in early June by green frogs and bullfrogs. Newts, active all spring, writhe and gyrate among the waterweeds as they court and gorge themselves on frog eggs.

Frogs and salamanders belong to an ancient group of backboned animals, the Amphibia, whose ancestors made their first appearance in the fossil record more than 350 million years ago, well before the age of dinosaurs. Of the Earth's approximately 2,000 species of frogs and 280 species of salamanders, 10 species of frogs and 9 species of salamanders are found in northern New England, and all except for the red-backed salamander are chained to the water for egg-laying and at least the tadpole stage of development. All can be counted on for a lively nuptial show, for which the frogs provide the music and the salamanders the rhythmic and sensual courtship dance.

Frogs were the first animals on the Earth to chart the unknown territory of vocal sound. For them, at least, not much has changed. They are still brought together at the breeding pools by sound. Males form the chorus. The females respond, selecting mates by the quality of their voices. A young male frog visiting the nuptial pool for the first time generates a higher-pitched sound than the older, larger adults. These juvenile croaks, with frequencies of five to six hundred cycles per second, are above the threshold of sound for mature frogs and block any response from the females. Unlike the deeper croaks of adults, they do not provoke other males to join in song. The young frogs' smaller mouth cavities and vocal cords separate the men from the boys, allowing only the fertile members of the coterie to meet and engage in connubial bliss. The call of each species is distinctive: wood frogs croak, peepers peep, American toads and gray treefrogs trill, leopard and pickerel frogs snore, mink frogs cluck, green frogs twang, and bullfrogs belch. Only among wood frogs do males choose their partners; in other species the female chooses a mate by the strength and resonance of his call.

Salamanders, by contrast, have no middle ear to receive sound. Bones in the backs of their jaws conduct low-frequency vibrations from the ground to the inner ear, from which they hear little more than the pulse of their immediate environment. And they have no vocal cords with which to produce sound. Their courtship is silent and is triggered by ritualized behavior and odor instead of sound. When April temperatures reach forty-five degrees, and a long rain extends into the evening, spotted salamanders are awakened by water trickling through the forest soil. They push their way up through the earth, and guided by gravity and a moisture gradient, they begin

25

their annual migration to our vernal pool. The big salamanders prefer these ephemeral woodland pools because they contain no fish, which prey on eggs, tadpoles, and adults. Once the six- to eight-inch spotted salamanders reach the water the dance begins.

The number of salamanders that can exist in a single pool is extraordinary. The pool behind our mailbox supports only five or six, so when I want to imbibe their primitive ritual I go to Goodrich Four Corners in Norwich. One spring a congress of more than seventy male spotted salamanders, their yellow spots gleaming in the beam of my flashlight, twisted and turned on a mat of drowned maple leaves. This congress had an agenda. When the first female arrived, she approached the group and picked a mate. The two swam away to a less crowded section of the pool and began to circle, cheek to cheek like spinning square-dance partners. The night was filled with the jarring sound of peepers and wood frogs gabbled like geese, but the salamanders, deaf to the noise, wagged their tails, rubbed their chins, and danced in silence.

When the male broke away I followed him with my light, in and out of the waterweeds to a shallower section of the pool. Here he deposited white conical packets of sperm — spermatophores — on the bottom of the pool. He interrupted this activity twice to rise to the surface for air, legs folded against his sides, propelled by his twisting body and tail. His strokes, not swift and precise like the newt's, were more lumbering and jerky, like a wind-up toy.

When the last spermatophore was in place he swam back to the female and coaxed her into the shallows, directly to the white packets. She straddled and picked up the spermatophores with the lips of her cloaca, consummating their courtship with this act of prepackaged sex. Retrieving the spermatophores is the closest thing to internal fertilization in the amphibian world, and it is perhaps the closest thing to human joy a salamander knows. By the time she was through the male had already returned to the congress, and the female, swollen with eggs and carrying sperm, swam off into deeper water, her yellow spots fading in my light beam. Hours later, as dozens of other pairs of spotted salamanders danced in the shallows, she gripped a submerged branch with all four feet, with her tail wrapped around once to anchor her. With her cloaca pressed against the branch, the salamander deposited an oval mass containing between twenty and forty eggs. Farther down the branch she placed another mass of eggs, and another.

As the eggs passed out of the female's cloaca, the spermatophores ruptured and fertilized them all. Soon the gelatinous envelope around each cluster of eggs absorbed water and swelled to the size of a lemon. If air is trapped inside the gel, the sac turns milky white. Sometimes the sacs turn bright green, with algae that grow on the outside of the eggs. The algae camouflage the developing embryos and provide them with a rich supply of oxygen, and thrive on the embryos' carbon dioxide and bodily wastes in return. Eggs coated with algae produce larger embryos, hatch earlier, and have a lower mortality rate than eggs without algae. When she finished attaching her eggs, the spotted salamander, now thin and effete, sank to the bottom of the pool. Several hours later, just before dawn and as the rain fell harder, she ambled out of some rank growth and swam toward the shore. I followed her with my flashlight as she went past the old broken stalks of sedge and cattail, out of the water, and into the woods. She had gone back into the earth to feed on beetle larvae and earthworms. Gone for another year.

When wood frogs reach the water all hell breaks lose. I heard my first frogs this spring on March 29 — two weeks earlier than usual — calling from the tiny willow-alder pool behind our mailbox. It was not a great gathering of anurans. Just four wood frogs, the vanguard of a chorus that would dominate the nights to come, blended their voices on an overcast afternoon. I stood on the porch and listened to them croak their primitive soundings. Their song was older than the song of birds, older than the hill upon which they live. There were just four frogs, but they were an irrevocable sign of the season, as much so as the first robin on the lawn or the first blue wisp of hepatica in the woods.

After a mild spring rain a week later, wood frogs gabbled from our pool like a flock of ducks. Ice and cold water were no bother to these frogs, which I've seen in tundra pools on the edge of

Hudson Bay. And they range even farther north, just beyond the Arctic Circle, farther than any other North American amphibian. I enjoy watching wood frogs court, for they play by different rules. Most female frogs wait demurely for the males to call them to the pools, but not the wood frog. Males and females reach the water at the same time. Males, aggregated in one or two small groups, begin calling as soon as they get their feet wet. They sprawl on the water, floating with their heads above the surface and their side throat pouches ballooning with air. So eager are the males to breed, they may pounce on anything that remotely resembles a female. On several occasions I have removed over-zealous male wood frogs from the backs of spotted salamanders, and once a desperate frog pursued and mounted my thumb.

Fertilization in frogs is external. During amplexus, the sexual embrace of frogs, the male — always the smaller of the two — climbs onto his mate's back and grips her behind the forelegs to force out the eggs, which he then sprays with sperm. The male is aided in amplexus by swollen thumbs. Once perched on the female's back, forelegs wrapped around her chest, he locks his thumbs together so that he won't be dislodged by competitors. Last year I watched as a female swam into a group of males and received the attention of two eager suitors. The first male to reach her engaged in amplexus, squeezing and squeezing as an egg mass began to protrude from her cloaca. Their constantly kicking hind feet rolled the egg mass into a ball and spread the male's seeds. When the second male frog grabbed her around the head, all three frogs thrashed about, the female depositing eggs, the first male fertilizing them, and the second making a general pest of himself. Eventually, the second male realized his folly and released the female's head. He swam to the nearest unclaimed frog, but that one, unfortunately, was another male. Annoyed by the uninvited attention, the third male grunted — a signal both males and spent females give to ward off sex-crazed males — and dove to the bottom of the pool.

A female wood frog lays as many as three thousand eggs, each individually encased in a gelatinous envelope that mats the entire clutch together. The egg masses, which are four or five inches across after absorbing water, are attached to grasses and twigs or are left to float free near the shoreline like globs of pond scum. Each embryo has a dark upper surface (collectively they pepper the surface of the otherwise translucent egg mass) that absorbs sunlight and speeds development. The adults are also dark on top to absorb heat, but under the summer sun their chromatophores spread apart, and except for a distinctive black mask, the adult wood frogs become a lighter, rich fawn brown. Within a week the breeding season of the wood frog is over, the pool behind the mailbox is deserted, and the only vestige of their passing is a thick, gelatinous mat of eggs that rims the shoreline and clouds the water.

Spring peepers are more sedate than wood frogs. Males call from the shoreline vegetation throughout our wetland and wait patiently for a female to initiate amplexus. The choice of an appropriately sized mate is essential to spring peepers and American toads, which, unlike other north country frogs, do not lay their eggs in masses. Instead, peepers attach their six hundred to twelve hundred eggs one at a time to submerged plants, and toads lay their eggs in long winding strings. If a male of either species is too large for the female, his vent will extend beyond his mate's and the sperm will miss the mark, the eggs going unfertilized.

One night in early May, after the wood frogs had left the water, I walked toward the marsh behind our garden where the peepers' electronic chorus was deafening. When I reached the edge of the water the peepers fell silent. Only the voice of distant pools, like the chime of sleigh bells, fed the night with sound. I waited briefly to let my presence fade from the frogs' feeble memories. In a moment one peeped from across the marsh, then another and another until my head swarmed with a sound so loud and piercing that it erased my thoughts. After several minutes I found one of the inch-long treefrogs calling from a broken cattail stem, where it clung with suction-tipped toes. He emptied his lungs of air and filled his vocal sac until the bubble protruding from his throat was bigger than his head. Air passing back and forth between lungs and vocal sac strummed the vocal cords on the floor of his mouth, and the vibrating sac acted as a resonance chamber to amplify the call. In a few minutes another

male wandered over and the two peepers began a duet, not the shrill mating call but a long volley of trills that means a territorial dispute. When the interloper left the trilling stopped, and the first male, victorious and energetic, resumed his clear, two-note peeps. No female responded, at least not while I crouched in the mud. But the peeper's innate persistance is always rewarded. His frenetic song will play night after night, week after week, until a female moves toward him. Then without haste, he will abandon his throne of mud and climb onto her back, forelegs clasped around her body.

As the water temperature rises the embryos complete development and hatch. The tiny wood frog and peeper tadpoles use their rasping mouthparts to scrape algae and protozoa from the stems and leaves of submerged plants. In late July, by the time the marshes and ephemeral pools are almost dry, metamorphosis is complete and half-inch wood frogs and peepers no bigger than houseflies head for the woods. From the moment the little frogs leave their nursery they are adept at walking and jumping, and the treefrogs at climbing. Not only can peepers leap farther than seventeen times their body length but they can also adhere to smooth surfaces. An adult peeper won't break any records with its one-and-a-half foot leap, but if Carl Lewis had the same relative ability the World Record long jump would exceed one hundred feet. Still, spring peepers are reluctant jumpers. They prefer to climb.

As the peeper chorus reaches a frantic pitch, dozens — no, hundreds — of frogs give the night their voice, and the cacophony seeps through the chinks in our log home. April music. Earth music. So loud, for so long, that it is a challenge to sleep.

By the middle of May, American toads raise their voices above the din of peepers, animating the darkness with one of the most pleasant sounds of spring. Their voice is nothing like the nasal bleats of the Fowler's toads that filled my boyhood. Each high-pitched call lasts as long as thirty seconds and contains as many as thirty trills a second. There is no way to separate the American toad's fluttering music into distinct trills; the duration between the vibrating sounds is too short and, besides, the night is too fine to subvert its ambience with mathematics. The males who sing these songs compete intensely for the attention of the less numerous female American toads, which do not breed every year. Collectively, the males' voices guide the females out from under our porch and out of our garden. The louder and longer a male trills, the more likely a female will hop his way.

As I approach our pond the toads stop singing. When I walk along the edge they hop into the water, swim out into a narrow arc, and return to shore three or four feet away from where I stand. It doesn't matter that I'm still here with headlamp beaming, camera flashing. If a toad starts crooning from across the pond the stimulation becomes too great even for a prudent toad, and the chorus resumes. Toads, too, engage in trilling duels. Once I watched a small male, sitting upright with face pointed skyward, as he trilled into the night. A second male joined in, a third, and a fourth. A larger toad hopped into my light beam and challenged the first, a smaller male. For several minutes they exchanged trills, then the smaller toad, whose voice seemed less potent in the presence of his challenger, fled the stage and disappeared into the dark water. Soon a female, almost five inches from nose to vent and much larger than the victorious male, left the wet meadow grass and moved straight to his calling station. Within a minute she was spoken for and mating began. The male perched on her back with his front legs wrapped around her chest and squeezed until two streams of eggs flowed from her body. The two toads moved as one, over and under submerged branches, as she fastened and he fertilized the long strings of eggs. Hours later, when the she was spent, the female left the pond. The male had other plans. He sent his voice, strong and sweet, back across the meadow to lure another mate. The night grew richer for his efforts.

By late May the chorus of American toads begins to fade and the gray treefrog raises his voice in song. On warm, humid nights I hear the males trilling from the saplings and mud flats around the peat pond. Their voices are harsher than those of the toads, a deep, masculine uvular trill. Gray treefrogs are much larger than spring peepers and have a warty back etched with irregular black lines. Their inner thighs are bright orange, and the base color of their backs can change from gray-brown to light green to pearly gray depending on the season and the habitat. I've caught gray-brown males along the pond shore where they blended into the muck. Those trilling from trees are gray-green. Later in June, when I catch treefrogs in my flashlight beam high in the aspens where they forage for insects, they are a bright green.

I've heard the treefrogs as early as May 23, calling from the shrubs along the Indian Springs. As the days grow warmer and the nights more humid, they follow the moisture gradient downhill and collect in a copse of willow, alder, and elm that flank the peat pond. When the treefrogs are on their calls are deafening. Early one June I went into the pond with hip boots and headlamp looking for frogs. Three males trilled from a tangle of willow trees, a counterpoint to the peepers that still chorused in the background. Finding the treefrogs was a challenge. As I hacked my way closer to the songs the frogs stopped. So I moved away from the brittle vegetation and into the shallows. Although the treefrogs resumed their chorus, I had made the wrong choice. Five feet from the shoreline I stepped into a soft spot and settled up to my waist in ooze. Filled with muck and water, my hip boots weighed a ton. My legs were anchored. I stretched my hands over my head to protect the camera and strobe light and sank deeper as the frogs sang on.

I hollered for Linny, who warm and comfortable chatted on the telephone, unaware that I was being swallowed. The more I yelled the more those frogs seemed to sing. There was no way she was going hear me over the amphibious cacophony. As I continued to sink I imagined our neighbor John towing me out with his tractor. Worse, I thought of the bog people of Ireland, the bones of mammoths and mastodons skewered by muck, and the tar pits of Rancho La Brea. I felt myself sinking away forever, a frog martyr fossilized within sight of his home. It was never like this back at the sump.

When I realized that John's tractor could not penetrate the wall of vegetation around the peat pond until late July, I removed my headlamp and placed my camera and strobe precariously on a hummock of marsh grass. There was nothing left to do but sprawl out as though as I was in quick sand and swim for shore. Like a worm I stretched out, inched my way toward an overhanging willow limb, grabbed on, and pulled. The limb snapped and I settled back into the ooze. Again I worked myself forward, grabbing the willow trunk this time. Thicker and less brittle, it held. The muck made obscene noises as my body slurped forward. The frogs sang on.

I returned to the peat pond two nights later with Linny as my coach. The chorus of gray treefrogs had swelled to fifteen, and the breeding season was in full swing. Most of the frogs had left the shrubs and trilled from the shore close to an old growth of cattails and rushes. Finding them was easier this time. The night was warm and, caught in their frenetic courtship, the treefrogs paid little attention as I bobbed up and down the shoreline. I found one male in a spit of cattails. Each time he trilled he filled his vocal sac with air, lifted his head toward the sky, and vibrated his entire upper torso. After each trill he lowered his head and waited. Whenever a neighboring frog sang he started up again. Then, after more than an hour of discordant music, a large gray female treefrog hopped over and stood on the male's back, choosing him over the six frogs in the adjoining chorus. The male moved out from under his bride, climbed on her back, and locked into amplexus. Together they sat, biding their time. Eventually the frogs piggybacked into the shallows. Almost as soon as they were gone another male hopped over and began calling from the exact spot the first male had left, as if that cattail spit was blessed.

Every spring I learn something new about the frogs. Last year I began visiting the pond at sundown, just before darkness settled on the valley. No treefrogs were in the water. They called from the elms, aspens, and red oaks thirty or forty yards from the shoreline. As the night congealed the treefrogs moved closer to the shore, jumping from tree to tree as though playing follow the leader. When a treefrog left one perch for another closer to the pond the next frog moved up from the back to take his place. The wave of frogs continued until the last one entered the water to secure a calling site or to wait in the wings for a successful male to leave with his bride.

35

When I was in grade school my mother kept a fifteen-gallon aquarium with four goldfish and two newts in the kitchen. The newts, natives of Long Island, were purchased at a local pet store to encourage my budding interest in amphibians. I fed them fish food and flies, pretended they were alligators, and brought them to the Beech Street Elementary School on pet day. When I reached college I caught my first wild newts in an Indiana pond. The pond was a breeding ground for a large and vociferous community of wood frogs whose eggs I had gone to collect. I couldn't resist the newts and placed three of them in a five-gallon jar with a mat of several hundred wood frog eggs. Instantly the newts pushed their way into the gelatinous mass, and began to gobble up the frog eggs. I was stunned. The next morning I brought my collection to the biology lab — three chubby newts and a handful of gelatinous mat.

Now when I want to watch newts feed, I walk down to the water as soon as the wood frogs gather and visit there periodically throughout the spring. Over a week's time their gelatinous egg masses stretch out several feet from the shoreline. Each April dozens of newts assemble along the shoreline and wait for the wood frogs to lay their eggs. Starting at the far end of the egg masses and working their way in, newts pluck the eggs from the gelatinous membranes one by one and the dark frog embryos vanish before my eyes. It is no wonder peepers hide their eggs one at a time. By placing their clutches together in large clumps, wood frogs ensure that many of the eggs will hatch due to their sheer volume. But newt predation is not limited to eggs. They devour tadpoles with equal gusto. Each spring I sit and watch newts eat wood frog tadpoles at the Montshire Museum's Ephemeral Farm, a series of five-gallon jars each housing a separate member of a woodland pool. Almost everyone in the farm dines on wood frog tadpoles, the meadow voles of woodland pools. The leech and giant water bug suck them dry; the dragonfly nymph and diving beetle chew them up piecemeal; and the newts, swift and accurate, practically inhale them.

The eastern red-spotted newt, *Notophthalmus viridescens*, is abundant in the Connecticut River Valley and is the most well known salamander in eastern North America. Of all the amphibians that gather in our wetlands, the newt has the most unusual life cycle. Adults and tadpoles are aquatic, but in its intermediate form, the red-eft stage, the newt is terrestrial and ubiquitous. After the tadpoles metamorphose as red efts, they crawl out of the water and head for the woods where they spend two or three years creeping about in the leaf litter. I find them beneath the woodpile, in the compost, under boards and mulch, on the lawn, and in the garden. And when it rains, efts are everywhere.

Once a tadpole becomes an eft it leaves the water to roam, a critical stage for the survival of the species. Red-spotted newts, during the past million or so years, have become beaver-pond specialists in the Northeast. Although they breed elsewhere, in lake margins, bogs, farm ponds, and sluggish streams, the red-eft stage, a unique occurrence among salamanders that is restricted to the genus *Notophthalmus*, is the newt's method for colonizing new beaver ponds. Because beaver ponds are transitory (most last from ten to twenty-five years) and because adult newts are restricted to water, a dried-up beaver pond means a dried-up newt. Without their nomadic land stage red-spotted newts could not exploit the work of beavers. On Long Island and elsewhere along the Middle Atlantic Coast beaver ponds are rare, so newts, confined to permanent marshes and sluggish rivers, skip the eft stage and transform directly from tadpoles to adults. In some locations metamorphosis is incomplete; the adult newts retain the long, branched gills of the larvae and never develop lungs. These newts are neoteric, sexually active although still bearing juvenile traits.

I saw my first eft sometime before my seventh birthday on a trail in the "borscht belt" of the Catskill Mountains. I wanted to take it home but my father, a pragmatist, thought the Wantagh Jewish Center's annual retreat was not the proper place for a boy and his amphibian. He and a another man told me that the little "red lizard" was poisonous. Now, my dad knows a lot about clothes and golf but he knows very little about things that crawl. Still, about the eft he was right. Their bright red color and warty texture make them easy to recognize. Like the distinctive stained-glass pattern of a monarch butterfly's wing, the red of the eft is a warning. They are unpalatable, poisonous. I have fed efts to a variety of predators, all with the same result. Barred owls spit them out. Opossums and skunks sniffed them and turned away. A green frog ate one and died. Even garter snakes, after exploring them with their tongues, passed them up. The snakes will, however, eat smooth-skinned, drab olive adult newts; I fed the two from my mother's goldfish bowl to Queenie. Otter, when pressed by hunger or boredom, will eat adult newts, but fish reject them.

From April through June I see the adult newts engage in their mating rituals, the male clutched high on the female's back, doubled over so that his chin rubs against hers. Together they dance, tails flailing and bodies entwined, as the male secretes hormones from the hedonic glands on his chin and smears them on the female's body. When their courtship is over the male deposits spermatophores and the female collects them in her cloaca. Each egg is placed singly on submerged vegetation, perhaps to hide them from their ravenous neighbors.

Like adult newts, green frogs and bullfrogs are permanent residents of our marsh and peat pond. Rarely do they leave the water. Their voices usher in summer and fade by August. On warm summer nights, when fireflies decorate the front yard, I listen for the twangs and grunts of these frogs rising from the pond. If the chorus is ripping, there will be plenty of action along the shoreline, for both bullfrogs and green frogs are territorial. Male bullfrogs stake out a parcel of pond and defend it against other male bullfrogs night after night, using their voice to proclaim occupancy and attract females in the same manner as male songbirds. Last summer, in the light of a half moon, I saw a bullfrog trespass on another's territory. The owner met the challenge full force. Eight times he inflated his lungs and guts, then leaped in the air, erect and bloated. A jolly shoving match ensued, with both squat frogs bouncing and grappling like Sumo wrestlers. To the victor — in this case the larger frog and resident landowner — went the spoils: the more prominent calling site. Sometimes, if the loser is small and careless, he may himself become part of the spoils and wind up in the belly of his assailant.

A female bullfrog must be equally careful when selecting a mate. If she chooses a male that exceeds her size she may end up defending herself rather than mating. The prudent female gauges the size of her suitor by the depth and resonance of his voice, approaching only those males whose dimensions are compatible with her own. Since green frogs rarely exceed four inches from nose to vent (bullfrogs grow to more than twice that size), the female's selection of an appropriately sized mate is not a life-or-death choice.

Unlike bullfrogs, male green frogs call while sitting in the shallows and never climb on rocks or floating debris to proclaim their territory. The peat pond is less than a tenth of an acre and supports only two or three bullfrogs; any more, and the herd of green frogs, which share the warm mud and dense emergent vegetation, would be reduced to a handful. Both species begin calling in late afternoon when the water temperature is close to seventy degrees and continue their serenade throughout the night. Although the bullfrog's voice carries farther — more than a quarter of a mile on still mornings — the green frog uses so much force in producing a call that its body rises out of the water and pitches forward with each twang. As the green frog jerks out of the water his bright yellow throat flashes. From across our small pond I can see a dozen green frogs idling in the muck, their heads just above the surface. One twangs, like a loose banjo string. Then another. The bullfrogs, more cautious, wait for me to stop moving before announcing their intentions.

In addition to their voices and the yellow throat of the male green frog, there is another characteristic that can be used to differentiate beween these two green-colored frogs: the presence or absence of the dorsolateral ridge. These ridges are parallel folds of skin that begin behind the eye and extend down the back like elevated stripes. Green frogs have them, bullfrogs do not. Both frogs attach their eggs to submerged vegetation. Because the water is warm, embryonic development is quick and the tadpoles hatch in less than two weeks. By the time the bullfrog and green frog eggs hatch, spring peepers have joined the wood frogs on the forest floor, gray treefrogs have returned to the trees, and American toads to the garden. Spotted salamanders, long gone from their vernal pools, lie hidden beneath the forest duff or in subterranean tunnels. Thousands of transforming amphibians, the products of another successful spring, tread through the waterweeds close to shore. As the summer sun shrinks their nursery, metamorphosis speeds up, and eventually a legion of froglets — their gills and tails gone, their lungs and legs working — hop tentatively onto the shore. A few days later the froglets, guided by instinct, move toward the habitat of their parents and begin a new life as voracious insect eaters.

The tadpoles of green frogs and bullfrogs require a longer time to transform than those of other northeastern frogs. Green frog tadpoles winter over and complete metamorphosis during their second summer, and bullfrog tadpoles, which grow to more than six inches long, may take up to three summers to develop into froglets. When metamorphosis is over, herds of small green frogs and bullfrogs station themselves along the shoreline and wait for unsuspecting aquatic insects — water striders, whirl-a-gig beetles, water boatman, and mayflies — while attempting to avoid the cavernous mouths of their parents. As the young of other frog species march out of the water, green frogs and bullfrogs wait by the most heavily used section of the shoreline. Froglet after froglet is gobbled up. It makes no difference whether it's a wood frog or peeper, American toad or gray treefrog; if it moves and if it's small enough, it's eaten.

Of all of our amphibians, the bullfrog has the most catholic diet. Any animal that moves and that can fit into its mouth is suitable food. So great is its appetite, a bullfrog can be thought of as a mouth and stomach propelled by huge hind legs. I have dissected bullfrogs and found their stomachs crammed with baby painted and snapping turtles, crayfish, dragonflies, and other frogs. I once watched a moderately sized bullfrog stuff a full-grown green frog in its mouth. For ten minutes the green frog struggled, its feet flailing from the bigger frog's mouth, until tired and deprived of air it relaxed, disappearing into the cavernous void. As soon as the bullfrog forced down its lunch, it stationed itself by the shoreline and waited for another victim. Even barn swallows and cliff swallows, which go to the shore to collect mud for their nests, and swamp sparrows, which stalk through the reeds, may wind up in the belly of a bullfrog. Unsuspecting hummingbirds sipping nectar from the blossoms of the jewelweed and cardinal flower are caught; so are meadow voles, water shrews, ducklings, and moderately sized snakes.

I know of no other animal whose voice, relative to its size, projects as far as that of the bullfrog's. When I was an Audubon Society naturalist in the midseventies, tracking fishers in southwestern New Hampshire, I lived at the Willard Pond Sanctuary, in Antrim, in a cottage next to a small millpond that was full of bullfrogs. Every evening the males climbed up on small boulders that were scattered around the shallows, one frog to a rock, and filled the night with sonorous calls. From a distance they sounded like a roll of summer thunder, it was so deafening. I was not the only one tuned to their clamor. A pair of barred owls regularly perched on snags and hunted frogs. By morning a red-shouldered hawk replaced the owls. A family of raccoons and an itinerant otter also used the pond as their larder and drove the frogs, leaping and squealing with terror, into the depths of the pond.

When cold weather approaches in October green frogs and bullfrogs settle into the mud on the bottom of the pond, their metabolism slowed to a tick. What little oxygen they require during hibernation is absorbed from the water through the lining of their skin. For terrestrial hibernating frogs — peepers, gray treefrogs, wood frogs, and American toads — life is more strenuous. The frogs that pass the winter beneath the leaf litter behind our cabin or in shallow burrows in the loose soil of our garden are subjected to freezing temperatures. To avoid freezing solid the land-based frogs produce glycerol, an alcohol used in several brands of commercial antifreeze. They also drain much of the fluid from their cells so that when ice does form it collects outside the cell membranes and does not damage the inner structure of the cell. If it were not for this capacity to tolerate partial freezing our wetlands would be silent. The spotted salamanders burrow below the frost line or work their way into the stone foundations of old farmhouses. Each winter I hear stories about these big salamanders hibernating in basements, motionless but alive. Newts stay under the ice, drugged by the cold, and tread water all winter.

During those rare times when cold weather comes before snow, I lay down on the black ice and watch newts move, each stroke lethargic and measured. In early October, a week after the first frost, Linny turned over the garden soil and a found fat wood frog six inches below the surface. Like a deciduous bud that developes in summer, endures winter, and unfurls in spring, this frog was already set for the first warm rain in April that will call her to the vernal pool behind our mailbox. Huddled in her icy burrow, she was swollen with eggs.

4

BLUEBIRDS

WHEN THE MALE BLUEBIRD FIRST ARRIVED in our front yard Linny and I adopted a new routine. Whoever reached the living room first would glance out the big window toward the north end of the garden, where a homemade birdhouse stood, and report on all aspects of the bird's behavior. Whether the bluebird perched on the birdhouse, stalked through the brown grasses along the edge of the garden fence, or caroled from the flowering crab — all this was grist for our mill.

To us he was the purest blue, bluer than the bluest May sky, and his residence in our garden gave us delight. It was the perfect place. The earth was brown and rich and would produce a bumper crop of insects. The grass on the western side of the garden was wild and untended, a perfect nursery for grasshopper nymphs and caterpillars. And when those pruning machines hopped, wiggled, and crawled over to the short grass on the eastern side of the garden, the bluebird would have an unobstructed view of his breakfast. To the south of the garden was a marsh bordered by red and black raspberry canes and patches of wild strawberries. Beyond the marsh were pin cherries and shadbush and a copse of aspen. There were enough berries and insects in our front yard for two broods of bluebirds, maybe three.

The bluebird was sleek and stoop-shouldered as he perched on the top of the birdhouse, a well-fed, well-feathered individual. His cheeks, head, back, wings, and tail were bright blue. His throat, breast, and flanks were reddish brown, the color of Georgia soil. His belly was white. He had a thin black bill and penetrating black eyes. His slightest movement caught our attention. He came to the garden from the south — Maryland, Delaware, maybe Virginia — and began to stake claim to the entire front yard. Our property was his, we decided, the first time we saw him. From his perch on the birdhouse or from high in the aspens, he watched our rusted Volvo limp out of the driveway and our perk little Toyota zip in. Nothing seemed to bother the bluebird, for he went about his business with complete confidence. Even our dog, whose wild peregrinations left ruts in the meadow, was just another attraction.

I don't remember who spotted the female, but when her identification was confirmed we spread the news like expectant parents. She was interested in the male's rich warble and his immaculate appearance, and in the birdhouse as well. It was the perfect place to live. For several days the bluebird attended his mate, bringing her tidbits from the meadow and the marsh. Each bird took turns inspecting the birdhouse. In an effort to ensure the bluebirds would remain with us for the spring, Linny assembled two more houses and tacked them twenty feet apart to the cedar fence posts on the west side of the garden. We now had four bluebird houses, more than enough to accommodate the bold tree swallows that had just arrived.

The female bluebird wasted no time in visiting the new houses. The old house on the south side of the garden closest to the marsh was never really a consideration. She checked it out once and never returned. The previous summer a pair of bluebirds had spent two days contemplating that house before disappearing for points unknown. This year we thought we'd hedge our bets with four houses, although I have a friend who stakes out at least a dozen nest boxes to secure a single pair of bluebirds in her yard.

44

How could we lose with four birdhouses? It was, after all, the perfect place to live.

Both birds brought grass stems into the north house. She did most of the work while he flitted from post to post and post to aspen and back again. Sometimes he stopped to sing three or four sweet gurgling notes, but more often he paraded around the front yard keeping a vigilant watch for tree swallows, house sparrows, and starlings. The entrance to the birdhouse was one-and-a-half inches in diameter, too small for a starling but just right for a tree swallow or house sparrow. There were no house sparrows around to challenge the bluebirds for possession of the north box. Tree swallows there were, plenty of them, but on cold mornings they left the area to feed closer to the Connecticut River. The bluebirds worked fast, establishing themselves before the swallows returned for good.

Then the bluebirds disappeared. I checked all four houses for clues. As I expected, the north-side house had a nest, a loose affair of grasses both coarse and fine shaped into a cup. There were no eggs. The birds returned two weeks later, and four days after that, on May 16, five pale-blue eggs — the palest of all eastern thrush eggs — filled the nest cup. For immediate neighbors the bluebirds had chickadees, which had picked a box on the west side of the garden. Their nest, a mass of soft sphagnum moss woven with strands of our dog's hair and shredded silk from moth cocoons, was a soft, comfortable-looking nest. Inside, six tiny white eggs speckled with rusty brown — each no bigger than my pinky nail — lay cradled in the moss.

Tree swallows constructed their nest — a rather shabby affair of dried grasses and chicken feathers — south of the chickadees and also on the garden's west side. They were the overlords of the neighborhood, chasing anything — bird or person — that approached their nest box. Linny and I were delighted, for only one box was vacant. Except for a gathering of earwigs, the house on the south side stood empty. Having acheived a 75 percent occupancy, we showered ourselves with accolades and boasted to everyone we knew who cared about birds of our great accomplishment.

The chickadees and the tree swallows fledged young. The chickadees sent five babies into our meadows and woods, the swallows four.

The bluebirds, however, the pride and joy of our garden, the very reason we had built and set out four nesting boxes, met with disaster, and it was all our fault. Someone — I prefer to think it was Linny, she prefers to think it was me — bumped the bluebird box while digging and rototilling the garden. With only one nail supporting the nest box against a cedar post — definitely my oversight — the box rotated 180 degrees on its axis. All five eggs cracked. And the bluebirds, after several hours of piteous searching, left.

The following spring, filled with promise and hope, was met by early rototilling and structurally sound support systems for all four nest boxes. All three species — the bluebirds, tree swallows, and chickadees — returned and each claimed a box. Their nest sites rotated so that each took a different box from the year before. The chickadees, which had lingered around the sunflower feeders since early winter, moved into the BAD BOX — the one that had housed the bluebirds the previous year. Both birds collected sphagnum from the peeper pond below the driveway, and although Linny and I placed big balls of dog hair on the porch the chickadees preferred to gather the hair, one strand at a time, from the dog's green carpet. Each afternoon for six or seven days around the third week in May the male and female reported for hair. It didn't matter that I stood several feet away watching, or that the dog slept on the carpet — the chickadees were singular in their quest. On May 25, one egg was in their nest cup. A week later, five. After the clutch was set the female incubated while the male, resolute and generous, brought food. On June 13, thirteen days after the last egg was laid, five little chickadees lighter and smaller than June bugs hatched. When the days were cool the female chickadee stayed with her brood while the male did all the providing. Both birds flitted about the yard when the weather was warm, gathering caterpillars and spiders and bark beetles. The family prospered. It was the perfect place to live. The swallows, which had been around the garden since the second week in May, chose the box the chickadees had used the year before. For them it was *ménage a trois*, two females and a male. Mating climaxed as the male, in high gear and equal to the task, serviced both females from any available platform: all four nest boxes, the cedar posts, the roof of our house, the electric line.

Sex in the bird world is a fleeting but oft-repeated event. I was reminded of this one morning when, as I gazed out the kitchen window, the tree swallows consummated their nuptial vows six times in five minutes. For most animals this is excessive if not exhaustive, but for many birds sexual congress is performed with the same gusto as all the other basic functions of their energy-intensive lives. Although males of the more primitive species — ostriches, storks, flamingos, and waterfowl among others — have a grooved erect penis that guides the sperm into the female's cloaca, most male birds lack a copulatory organ. For lack of a better name, ornithologists refer to this penisless impregnation of the female as the "cloacal kiss."

The male swallow stood on one of his concubine's back, and the two birds positioned themselves so their cloacae touched. The process entailed a bit of avian gymnastics; the female had to raise her tail and twist her abdomen to the side so the cloacal openings could meet. In a moment it was over. Mating took place four times on the garden fence, twice on the birdhouse. Although each union lasts less than three seconds, a prodigious amount of sperm passes from the male to the female. More than 200 million sperm, like armies of microscopic tadpoles, enter the cloaca of a domestic pigeon per ejaculation; in chickens, the number approaches 8 billion.

Depending on the species, mating takes place on the ground, in the nest or nest box, in trees and bushes, on electric lines, in the water, or in the case of some species of swifts, in the air. A few birds are quite particular about where they bring courtship to fruition. Loons choose the edge of their nest, which has resulted in an unusual adaptation for a species of black fly. Male loons must be either very sloppy or suffer from premature ejaculation, for a host-specific species of black fly, attracted by the semen scattered over the nest, remains in the vicinity and dines on loon blood during the bird's twenty-eight-day incubation.

To limit weight as an aid in flight the reproductive organs of birds are reduced in size during most of the year. The testes may be two or three hundred times larger during the breeding season (in ducks they reach one-tenth of their body weight), and in most species the female's right ovary and oviduct are vestigial while the functional left side of the reproductive tract is nearly invisible during the off-season. The reduction of the ovaries from two to one not only eliminates unnecessary weight, but it also protects the developing eggs. For instance, if a female tree swallow experiences a rough landing, eggs housed side by side in parallel oviducts might meet and crack.

Linny and I once watched a pair of belted kingfishers mate. The female sat on a branch over the Ompompanoosuc River eating a crayfish while the male darted back and forth around the shoreline, rattling like an old alarm clock. When he felt the impulse, he flew over and landed on the female's back. Both birds positioned their tails so that their cloacae met, then the male, in a display of unmitigated passion, yanked on his mate's crest and consummated the act. Three times the birds mated, and each time the male pulled back on the female's crest. The tree swallows, crestless, just flicked their wings to maintain their balance. The one thing the tree swallows and the kingfishers did have in common was their lack of shame. They were exhibitionists, in the garden and by the river.

The two female tree swallows brought grasses and feathers to the nest box and placed them on top of a pile of sphagnum moss — a false start by the chickadees — then the trio disappeared. A few days later seven pure white eggs, each the size of my thumbnail, filled the nest cup. Like the chickadee, the female tree swallows did all the incubating. The male divided his time between the garden and the pond, seining insects from the air. The nest box the tree swallows had used the previous year was empty. The bluebirds, which had been in and out of the garden for three weeks, took the box on the south side that had gone unused the year before. In front of their nest box, between a narrow strip of lawn and a small cattail marsh, is a weeping willow. The willow was the bluebirds' favorite perch. Whenever I wanted to find the birds, I checked the willow first. Both the male and female hunted from the tree, dropping to the lawn for grasshoppers and crickets, or after a rain, for worms. In late afternoon they convened in the willow to preen. And every once in a while the bluebirds went to the willow, perched for a spell, then disappeared over the aspens beyond the south end of the garden.

The bluebirds were less conspicuous than the tree swallows and chickadees. Some days I never saw them. Most days I never heard them. I didn't mind, though; five eggs, pale-blue and warm, rested in the nest cup. For the next two weeks whenever Linny and I passed along the south side of the garden we held our breath. Then on June 18 — thirteen days after the clutch was completed — five baby bluebirds broke through their egg shells. We were ecstatic.

Each morning for the next twelve days I watched the bluebirds harvest insects from the front yard, the backyard, and the garden. Sometimes they'd perch on a garden fence post with heads tilted toward the ground. If a grasshopper leaped, a bluebird would drop into the timothy and hawkweed like a kestrel after a mouse. From midmorning on one of the two birds, usually the female, hunted grasshoppers and beetles from the electric line on the north side of the house. From that lofty height a bluebird could see down the driveway to the edge of the garden and across the side yard to the asparagus patch. Any insect that landed in the driveway was fair game. When I sat at my desk to write I had an unobstructed view of the line and could keep abreast of the bird's activity. From that upstairs window I watched her day after day like a cat staring into a goldfish bowl. Although the ground was out of my range of view, I could guess when the bluebird caught an insect. If her pounce was successful three or four minutes would elapse before she returned to the line. If she missed her insect she was back in view in a moment. To test my hypothesis, I rushed downstairs once or twice a day to watch the nest box. Each time, I found the bluebird standing on the garden fence or on the box with an insect in her bill.

After feeding the chicks the bluebird would probe around the nest until she found a white membranous fecal sac. The sac was always removed, sometimes eaten. Nest sanitation reduces odors that attract predators like squirrels and weasels and assures that the young birds do not soil their developing feathers. In the early stages of the chicks' growth the fecal sac contained undigested nutrients from which the adults derived some nourishment. As the young birds grew their digestion improved. The bluebird then retrieved the sacs, flew a short distance from the nest, and dropped them in the front yard. When her domestic chores were through, she returned to the electric line.

Once, when it rained so hard that the tree swallows and chickadees stayed at home, the male bluebird spent the afternoon catching earthworms. He flew behind the house to where the lawn meets the woods and stood on the edge of our hammock, where he was shielded from the wind and driving rain by an aspen canopy. Whenever an earthworm broke the surface the bluebird was there. He left the really large worms for the robins, selecting only those that fit comfortably in his bill.

Once in a while the bluebirds hunted like flycatchers — but more slowly — darting into the air after sluggish moths and crane flies. Or just above the top of the meadow they'd hover, snapping at anything that left the grass. Swift-flying insects like dragonflies and bees are too fast for bluebirds, but lethargic ones — froghoppers and leafhoppers, stinkbugs and spittlebugs — were snatched in midflight. And when the mayflies emerged from the pond behind the willow, the bluebirds were there. Trees, too, were methodically searched for insects. Both bluebirds had a knack for finding caterpillars and small katydids on the backs of leaves. The weeping willow in front of their nest box was a favorite. So were the aspens behind our house and the box elders along the driveway. There was no shortage of protein. And for a change of pace there were Juneberries and honeysuckle berries at the edge of the meadow. Beneath the wands of grass grew tiny wild strawberries.

When the black raspberries along the edge of the marsh ripened, the birds were there, for bluebirds, along with robins, cedar waxwings, catbirds, and all five species of thrushes, are the major fruit-eating birds of eastern North America. Fruit-eating birds and fruit-producing plants are entwined in a profitable relationship based on the birds' need for food and the plants' need for seed dispersal. After a bluebird digests the fleshy portion of the raspberry the seeds pass unharmed through its intestines and are defecated some distance from the parent plant. This movement of the seed benefits the raspberry, for any seed germinating beneath the mother plant competes for water, sunlight, and nutrients with a plant whose roots are deeper, branches longer, and leaves fuller and more numerous than the germinating seedling's. And since birds scatter seeds in small amounts, the seeds are less likely to be eaten by small mammals. To attract bluebirds and other fruit eaters and to cut down on wasted seed production — fruits that rot on the stem or are eaten by mice — black raspberries use a "preripening fruit flag" — that is, they go through a double color change before maturing. Green at first, black raspberries turn red before turning purple. They thus catch the eye of a bluebird before the fruit is mature, alerting the bird to the imminent availability of ripe fruit.

I had checked the box the day the chicks hatched. Five baby bluebirds, gray like mice, were bunched together in the nest cup. Their eyes were closed, their feathers sparse and fluffy. But when I scratched the box their little heads shot up, mouths agape and flashing a deep, bright yellow — perfect targets for a moveable feast. The chicks prospered. In five days their eyes opened and from that point on their response to me was lukewarm. After the eighth day they cringed in the nest cup whenever I paid them a visit. The adult bluebirds were just as wary. Unlike their neighbors, the tree swallows and chickadees who sat tight with their brood whenever I inspected the box, the bluebirds bolted before the door opened. Even at night, when I dumped the compost, the male or female spooked.

By day sixteen the chicks were close to fledging. As soon as the brood is out of the nest the male takes charge, while the female disappears to build a new nest. After the chickadees fledged I cleaned out their nest box to entice the female bluebird to stay in our garden. The female builds her second nest (or refurbishes the first one) alone, then lays a clutch of eggs and begins to incubate. All in a few days. For bluebirds there exists a close-knit family life. By the time the second brood is hatched the young of the first brood are grown. The male, now relieved of the responsibility of attending the first brood, can help the female collect insects and fruit for the new chicks. The fledglings, which often remain in the proximity of their nest, join their parents in feeding the second brood of young.

On day seventeen, however, tragedy struck. Shortly after the sun arched above the Connecticut River Valley, shortly after the bluebirds began to collect slow, dew-covered insects, a small thin mammal — perhaps a weasel — squeezed into the nest box. I checked the box at 7:00 A.M. and found a pile of blue-gray wing feathers — the lower vanes still pressed in their sheaths — some breast down, two feet, and the headless carcass of a chick opened lengthwise down the breast, the vital organs removed. A pair of virgin wings hung from the carcass.

We were devastated, but the adult bluebirds took this loss in stride. There was no piteous mourning. They stayed by the electric line collecting insects in the usual manner — dropping to the lawn, to the woodpile, to the driveway — but without chicks to feed, they returned to the line and consumed their catch. For more than a month I saw the bluebirds flitting around the front yard, from the garden to the willow to the flowering crab, harvesting insects and fruit. There was plenty of food.

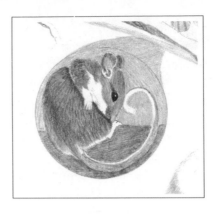

5

THE LIFE AND TIMES
OF A SHORT-TAILED WEASEL

I STOOD STILL AS THE WEASEL RIPPLED, white and lustrous, through the stonewall, her cold green eyes shining with a singular purpose: a moonlight hunt. Six feet away the deer mouse whose footfalls had aroused the weasel cowered against a tussock of grass. Suddenly it burst several feet to the right, then froze. Stung by the sound, the weasel hit the ground in a dead run. She held the mouse's convoluted trail with her nose to the earth like a bloodhound, twice passing within inches of the mouse itself. But the mouse never flinched, so the weasel pressed on. As she reached the last length of trail the mouse bolted. Simultaneously, the weasel screeched — a high-pitched noise that left her lungs momentarily airless — and continued the pursuit, a tiny warrior with inexhaustible concentration. The mouse, shadowed by the weasel, entered the wall and bounded from rock to rock then went off into a wand of tall grass. The weasel leaped, a thin bit of luminescent white. They darted across a mat of brittle leaves, across a shag of fern, along a length of fallen elm limb. Both animals merged in a blur, the weasel furiously kicking and scratching and wrapped snakelike around the mouse. When teeth met skull with an audible crunch, all struggling ceased, and the weasel, with prey in mouth, disappeared back into the stonewall.

I pursed my lips and squeaked, hoping to call the weasel back for an encore. But only the wind stirred, so I latched the pen and walked back toward the house.

Each spring Linny and I become surrogate parents to orphaned and injured wildlife. Our role is as set and predictable as a pair of orioles in an old elm. To date we've raised two red foxes, four mink, four skunks, a fisher, two opossums, a deer, two woodchucks, a porcupine, two barred owls, three saw-whet owls, two kestrels, two crows, and countless small rodents — red, gray, and flying squirrels, voles, and mice. None has been as rewarding and none has stayed as long as the short-tailed weasel that moved in early one May.

For me, raising and rehabilitating native wildlife is a pleasure. I enjoy observing animals in proximity and look forward to unraveling some of the mysteries of behavior peculiar to each species. Since my eighth birthday, when I received my first copy of Zim and Hoffmeister's *Golden Guide to Mammals* and discovered two paintings of a short-tailed weasel — one brown, the other ermine white — I wanted to learn more about this diminutive predator whose color and name change with the seasons. My wish came true twenty-eight years later when a distressed woman called the Montshire Museum to report that an orphaned weasel, blind and helpless, had been found. Linny and I drove down Greensboro Road to the outskirts of Hanover and the Berrill Farm. Four cars blocked the driveway. The woman who answered the door was much relieved that "the museum" had arrived. With rapt concern, five neighbors huddled over a cardboard box in the kitchen, debating the animal's chance of survival. The prognosis was slim for the infant weasel, which was chilled and starved and barely moving.

Three hours earlier the animal was found piteously chirping by the mouth of a burrow. Other burrows honeycombed the meadow, the woman said: the weasel mother's network, stolen from a chipmunk or a mole since weasels don't dig, was where she nursed her kits, cached food, and rested. The burrows all looked dormant. The woman had left the kit, hoping its mother would return, but by sunset the weasel was still chirping, and without help it would die. Linny and I took the kit and arranged a little weasel water bed — a large, durable zip-lock plastic bag half-filled with warm water and wrapped in a T-shirt — and packed both in a small cardboard box. The kit immediately burrowed into the shirt, curled up, and fell asleep. It awakened half an hour later, warm but hungry. Linny heated a plastic dropper filled with formula — a concoction of milk, instant baby cereal, and corn syrup — and gently squeezed the broth into the weasel's mouth. One drop, two drops, three drops. Dinner ended.

We tucked the weasel back into the T-shirt, insulating its water bed in a down jacket jammed inside a sleeping bag. Three hours later I awoke to a barrage of shrill chirps; the weasel was hungry, and its bed was cool. Half-asleep, I walked downstairs to the kitchen, the brooding mother hen, to begin a twice-nightly feeding routine that continued for more than two weeks. In the morning I read about postnatal development in the three species of North American weasels and decided ours was a short-tailed, *Mustela erminea*. The tip-off was a heavy brown mane over the forehead and shoulders. Visible after the first week, prominent after the second, eclipsed by surrounding fur after the fifth, the mane was a grip for the mother and for me. Since its teeth had erupted and it was more than four inches from nose to vent, the kit was two weeks old, I concluded.

Compared with most other mammals, weasels are born premature, almost embryonic. For three more weeks the kit lived behind a veil of darkness, its ears closed and tuned to the rapid pulse of its own heart. A longer, fuller uterine development would be a lethal burden to the mother, who, normally lithe and serpentine, would stick like a cork in small burrows. Although both the short- and long-tailed weasel — the two species indigenous to New England — have a nine-month gestation, implantation of the fertilized ovum is delayed for eight months, leaving only twenty-one to twenty-six days for uterine development, followed by a prolonged infancy.

Delayed implantation evolved independently through a number of lines of mammals, including bears, seals, bats, marsupials, armadillos, some species of deer, and most members of the weasel family, Mustelidae. For the short-tailed weasel, I see clear advantages. Heat comes in July before the now grown young disperse, making it easier for a male to find a mate. Once the female and her cluster of young are found, the quixotic male showers her with gifts: deer mice and voles and chipmunks. With this windfall a mother weasel can spend less time hunting and more time mating. The male not only mates with the mother but also with her female offspring. After a week or so of food delivery and mating the male leaves, and in his wake are pregnant mother and daughter weasels. Because delayed implantation keeps the fertilized eggs out of the uterus for eight months, yearling females mate their first summer (males their second), and so for the price of one courtship an adult male collects several mates. By bringing food to the mother weasel and her kits the male, even though he may not be their father, contributes to the fitness of an unborn generation.

The following day we switched the kit to kitten-milk substitute and watched with a sense of parental pride as it slowly increased its intake of food. Eight days later the little weasel began to fill out. Brown fur covered its top, white its bottom, and the tip of its tail turned black. Since weasels are sexually dimorphic — males that are up to twelve inches long (including a three-inch tail) and weigh four ounces, are about 30 percent larger than females, a trait first manifested during the fourth week — by the end of May I was convinced we had a female. With this in mind, we called her Weas. By the end of the fourth week her mane had disappeared, hidden in a robe of dense fur, and her diet had changed. Along with milk substitute, each feeding included bits of chicken liver, which she lapped and nipped from our fingers. Whenever Weas ingested a stringy piece she writhed and gyrated, scratching at her throat until the liver dislodged. In an emergency I once stuck my fingers tweezerlike down her throat to grab a long, twisted piece of connective tissue that had blocked her breathing. After each feeding — there were now four a day — she bolted down a half-dropper of formula.

On May 27, after having bulged beneath their lids for days, Weas' eyes, black and glistening like two beads of obsidian, opened on the world for the first time. With a squeak and a chirp she waddled into my palm, ready to be fed. Afterward I introduced Weas to Linny and the dog, who with two quick sniffs decided that eyes or no eyes, he was still bored. Although the dog wasn't impressed, we were. With her eyes now open Weas completed a vital transformation and became a creature with a personality. She was more active and vocal, and the muscles in her hind end began to develop. A week later she launched into a period of perpetual motion, so I moved her into a thirty-gallon aquarium with a carpet of pine needles and bark, branches and rocks to climb, and a bowl of water for drinking and bathing.

At nine weeks old Weas became interested in eviscerated mice. Abandoning both milk and liver, she ate only the most tender portions of the mice. By the second half of June she dissected them herself, eating everything but the long bones, tail, and hide. She made her first kill, four baby deer mice that had been collected by a friend, by the end of the month. Weas ate the tiny mice as though they were balls of meat with fur. Starting at the head and working back, she consumed everything. In spite of having no role model to mimic, no practice lessons with crippled prey, she pursued adult mice a week later. With newly sharpened reflexes and teeth and blind determination, Weas had become a predator. As her constant chatter and curiosity were part of her heritage, the products of eons of mustelid evolution, so was the wrapping of her body around prey and the lethal bite at the base of the skull.

Mustelids descended from a group of small, primitive predatory mammals, the *miacids*, during the late Eocene epoch, 38 million years ago, back when Old Faithful spewed lava, not steam. Although the miacids sired all seven families in the order Carnivora, the weasels were the first to diverge, though they retained many primitive characteristics: smallness, five-toed feet, and a penchant for forest dwelling. Most mustelids are long and thin and have short, stocky legs — two other miacid traits — that send them rippling over the landscape. Because they are built alike they have a tendency to move alike. Except for the skunk, which plods along grubbing for insects, mustelids leave a twin-print pattern like a sinuous trail of equal signs. With each bound Weas' body came together like an inch worm's, then sprang out. As she hit the ground, her hind feet landed in and usually obscured the prints of her front feet. The weasel family, which in the Northeast includes the mink, the otter, the striped skunk, the fisher, and both species of weasels, has another characteristic: anal scent glands. Most mustelids dabble the musk from their glands a little bit here and there along established trails to attract mates, set boundaries, and repel interlopers. Sometimes Weas sprayed, not a vile musk like a skunk, but a sweeter, earthier odor that told me she had been startled or was annoyed.

As a group mustelids have few rivals in their ability to stir the human imagination. Unfortunately, most of the tales they have engendered aren't true. Neither the long-tailed nor the short-tailed weasel sucks blood and neither is bloodthirsty. Although she occasionally bit the fingers that fed her and often licked the wounds of her victims, Weas was a predator like an owl or a cat, not a vampire. Fishers don't leap from trees onto the backs of deer and horses and they don't wait behind houses to steal cats and dogs. They do depend on deer meat in winter, but the deer they eat are already dead. The sound of barking dogs will send a fisher up a tree. Skunks can spray when suspended by the tail, but if the musk gets in your eyes you will not become permanently blinded.

Even the playful otter has been credited with some unusual feats. None, however, compares with the 1977 Animal Control Agents' Report for Hanover. Listed last, below 961 animal complaints — including one gerbil bite and two runaway jackasses — was a note that read: "Investigated a report of an otter chasing a mailman." Animal Agent Stan Milo confirmed the report that he had received a call from a distraught mail carrier who took refuge in somebody's house after being chased down the street by an otter. Milo followed up on the report and arrived in time to see the otter crawl back into Mink Brook. The post office offered no comment. E.B. White did, though. When my friend sent the report to *The New Yorker*, White responded, "Maybe that's what the Postal Service needs."

Even mustelid names add color to our language. You can "weasel" out of responsibilities; get "skunked" in sports; "ferret" out the facts; "badger" your parents; smell like a "polecat", and when smitten with lust have the sexual appetite of a "mink". When Teddy Roosevelt referred to the ambiguous language of politics, he referred to it as "weasel words."

In early August Weas outgrew the aquarium. She needed a spacious enclosure, one that would give her plenty of nooks and crannies to explore. A friend handy with a hammer and nails designed and built a twelve-by-six-by-five-foot hardware cloth pen and a plywood tunnel with a tiny nest chamber at one end. I did the interior decorating, lining the chamber with dried grass and fur, and buried the nest three feet below the ground with the tunnel entrance opened to the surface. Behind the tunnel I built a stonewall with dozens of rock shelves and small spaces, and behind that planted tussocks of grass and meadow perennials. Across the wall, broken tree limbs added another dimension to Weas' explorations. I hid the tunnel entrance with a curved sheet of maple bark, added more tussocks of grass, more tree limbs, and several wheelbarrow loads of pine needles for the floor. Except for the needles the front of the pen was bare so that I, too, had room to maneuver.

Weas took to her new home like a fish to water. Over and under and inside the stonewall, down the limbs, up limbs half-hidden by an arch of grass stems she flowed. Short-tailed weasels follow their own circuits, covering territories as large as fifty acres every week to ten days. Males keep large territories within which several females maintain overlapping home ranges. Compared to her wild relatives Weas was sedentary, however. Within the seventy-two square feet of floor space, the obstacles, and the hardware cloth frame, she expressed her nature. Mouse hunting was harder in the pen than in the aquarium, but whenever I released one Weas was up to the challenge. She employed all her senses in the hunt, first her ears then her nose. When she saw movement she rushed headlong after it, chattering and hyperventilating as though she was possessed. Weas drove her first mouse up the pen, grabbed its tail, and dropped down into the grass. Most mice were caught near the stonewall. Providing Weas with food was a chore. Every evening I set live traps near our compost pile, in the thickets by the peeper pond, and in the woods behind the house. Energetic predators like weasels are peripatetic; if they don't move around from place to place, a once-fertile hunting ground quickly becomes sterile. As the supply grew thin on our property, I trapped down by Webster Road around cellar holes and old stone foundations. When cold weather came and the mice moved indoors, I went with them, setting my traps, to our neighbors' delight, in their houses and barns.

Since weasels are quintessential mouse predators, they sometimes follow their prey into rural homes. During the blizzard of 1978, thirty-four inches of snow sent mice into cupboards, pantries, and root cellars. Weasels followed. I live-trapped one behind a refrigerator in Norwich, another by a stove in West Hartford, a third in a basement in Enfield. In all three homes they had cached excess food — mice and voles and scraps of meat — behind ranges and under sinks. In West Hartford, one weasel, after eliminating all the mice, subsisted on strips of liver. He would nervously accept the meat from the kids' fingers then dart behind the stove to dine in seclusion.

St. Johnsbury, Vermont, is a small urban island replete with red sandstone buildings, marble stairs, and gargoyles, anchored in a sea of rural poverty between rolling hills to the west and the Connecticut River to the east, sixty-five miles north of Hanover. It is the unofficial capital of Vermont's Northeast Kingdom, the home of a trucking company that bears the city's name, and a fine Victorian natural science museum, the Fairbanks. St. Johnsbury is also a city with weasels. Last winter several residents reported ermines in their homes. The Fairbanks Museum explained in each case that the fall of 1985 produced a bumper crop of mast (acorns and beechnuts) and seeds. And after a high production of nutritious food there follows a high production of nutritious mice. When the mouse population is up, more weasels survive the winter. Since a weasel can go absolutely anywhere a mouse can go, if snow forces mice inside, hungry weasels will follow. After rendering this snippet of natural history, the museum lent afflicted members Hav-a-hart traps.

One man caught an ermine and released it on the hill behind his house. The next night it was back. He reset the trap, and caught the weasel. This happened again and again. Eventually, he drove the weasel 6 miles away and released it. That night, the man again caught a weasel. He was sure it was the same one he had released. Of course no one believed him — a small mammal only twelve inches long cannot cover 6 miles in a single night, traveling past a corner of St. Johnsbury, over hills and forests and fields, past owls and cats and cars. The man was not convinced, so the next night he marked the weasel with a spot of green nail polish and again released it 6 miles from home. In the morning he checked the trap and found a weasel — ermine white with a black-tipped tail, a green spot on its rump. After notifying the Fairbanks Museum, he drove the weasel to the other side of St. Johnsbury, 12 miles away, and set it free. Although the record for the longest distance traveled by a short-tailed weasel is 21.6 miles, that record trip required seven months. The St. Johnsbury weasel didn't return.

The immature deer mice, although full-grown, lacked predator-avoidance skills. When Weas rushed along their trail the young mice flushed, while older mice held tight until the last minute. Every day we released a mouse or tossed in a section of a DOR (dead on road) chipmunk or squirrel. To keep the meat fresh I sectioned and served the squirrels over several days. When it was mealtime I stepped into her pen, rattled the stonewall as though knocking at her front door, and waited. Sometimes Weas slept so deeply it took several rattles to arouse her. She would always awake energized, then climb the wall and stand on her hind legs, looking over the spikes of grass. Once spotting me, she would run straight for me, jump on my pants, and race over my body. If I sat down, she'd roll over on her back and spar with my fingers, kicking and hissing. At the sight of food all games stopped. She'd screech, grab the meat, and recede to her lair beneath the wall. Twice I released a chipmunk in her pen with the same results. Weas engaged in a joust, screaming and casting musk, casually chasing her quarry around the pen. Although stockier and heavier than a female short-tailed weasel, the chipmunk was terrified. Once they surprised each other in the stonewall and bolted out opposite ends. A male weasel has little trouble dispatching a chipmunk, but for Weas this was her limit.

When I went to bed the first chipmunk was still in the pen. At 2:00 A.M. I was awakened by a demonic scream followed by silence. Then another scream. One of the two animals was dead. In the morning, I rattled the wall and the weasel appeared. The second chipmunk was also killed at night, but not before Weas had ripped all the skin off its tail in an attempt to work toward the head, leaving bone and red meat. I told my friend Sandra — an energetic naturalist who feeds wild mammals like most people feed birds — about the chipmunk's tail. She wasn't surprised, she said. The previous winter, a long-tailed weasel lived in her basement and preyed on rodents at the feeder. Throughout the winter Sandra encountered deer mice, chipmunks, red and flying squirrels with no fur on their tails. Once she watched the weasel grab a red squirrel by its tail and strip the skin and fur off it as the squirrel broke free, leaving the weasel with what looked like a limp party favor in its mouth.

Of the three species of North American weasels, the long-tailed weasel, *Mustela frenata*, is the largest. Males are eighteen inches long, including a six-and-a-half-inch tail, and weigh about eight ounces. In Vermont, females are four inches shorter and less than half as heavy. Besides leopards in the Old World, mountain lions in the New World, and man in both worlds, long-tailed weasels have the most extensive north-south distribution of any wild mammal. From southern Canada to Peru, they pursue rats, mice, squirrels, gophers, rabbits, and sometimes day-old piglets.

To look at drawers of study skins of these weasels in the American Museum of Natural History — the trays of each drawer representing a different geographic race or subspecies — is to almost hear Darwin think. From north to south, their color progressively shifts from dark to light to dark and back to light again. In Vermont, for instance, long-tailed weasels in their summer pelage are a uniform

dark-brown above and white below, similar to Weas; in southern Georgia and Florida they are lighter and have white facial markings; and weasels in Arizona, New Mexico, and Nevada are the lightest of all, with dark masks like black-footed ferrets. Farther south, into Mexico and Guatemala, weasels retain some white facial markings, but the light brown of the head and shoulders darkens to chocolate. In Panama, long-tailed weasels have no white on their faces at all, and their upper bodies are a uniform dark brown, almost black. Farther south still, they lighten again.

If one overlays the subspecies on a weather map, as E. Raymond Hall of the University of Kansas did, a pattern emerges: the color of long-tailed weasels follows a rainfall and humidity gradient. Weasels from the dank jungles of southern Central America are darkest, those from the deserts and grasslands the lightest. To the north and south of these points weasels are intermediate in color. After rearing humid-zone weasels in arid regions and visa versa, Hall determined that the color pattern cannot be changed within a few generations and therefore must be genetically set.

Hall also had something to say about the winter color of long-tailed weasels. Southern weasels molt in autumn, but not to white; northern weasels become ermines; and a geographical zone exists within which some weasels turn white and others do not. This equivocal zone extends across North America from south-central British Columbia, south in the mountains to the southern edge of the Sierra Nevada, and east across Arizona, New Mexico, and Texas. In southeastern Colorado the band widens and veers northeast into southern Vermont and southern New Hampshire. Within the band, males with brown winter coats and males with white coats are found in the same places. All females in the northern quarter of the band, however, turn white, and all females in the southern quarter remain brown in winter. Above the band, all long-tailed weasels molt to white, and below it all remain brown.

On Long Island long-tailed weasels are brown in winter, as they are throughout most of their extensive geographical range. In northern New England they are all ermines — or so says Hall's theory. But nothing in nature is ever as clear-cut and simple as it seems. Bands and lines of demarcation shimmy and shake by the century and the decade, and correlations are at best just handles with which scientists work. There are contradictions and exceptions and more shades of gray than are found in Ansel Adams' zone system. I was reminded again of this fact one December morning as I drove south on Route 302 along the flood plain of the lower Ammonoosuc River, which empties into the Connecticut below Woodsville. Less than a hundred yards from the main intersection in Lisbon, New Hampshire, I saw a small dark mammal curled in a ball, frozen solid. Another DOR. A red squirrel, I thought. I stopped the car, pulled off the road, and when the coast was clear backed up in the road-kill retrieval lane (sometimes referred to as the birding lane). If the animal was in mint condition and not squashed I would give it to the Montshire Museum for its mammal collection. If it was damaged I'd feed it to Weas. But to my delight and surprise, the DOR was neither squashed nor a squirrel. It was a weasel, a male long-tailed weasel — brown on top, white on the bottom — in its summer color but with thick, soft, fully winterized fur, and two hundred miles north of Hall's transcontinental band.

With short-tailed weasels, the coloration situation is not as complicated. They are circumpolar, ranging throughout northern Eurasia and Canada, south into the northern tier states, and into the mountainous West. Most but not all short-tailed weasels turn white in winter. On the British Isles, where snow is rare, most remain brown, and the one Long Island specimen I found at the American Museum of Natural History, collected in mid-November 1907, was also brown. In both species of weasel decreasing daylight triggers the autumn molt. The timing, however, is seldom precise and varies between species, within each species, and even from year to year in the same individual. As nights grow longer, days shorter, and the maple begins to blush, the diminished light falling on a weasel's eyes cause the pituitary gland — the body's master chemist — to signal the pineal gland. In most northern weasels the pineal gland secrets melatonin, which alerts the central nervous system to stop the production of melanin, a dark pigment found in hair follicles. Thus, new hairs turn white.

On the last day of September I noticed that, like a light dusting of snow on open ground, some white hairs had crept up Weas' sides. Day by day the white spread over her legs, face, tail, and up her back. By mid-October she was all white except for the nape of her neck and the tip of her tail, which remains black all winter to trick predators — hawks, owls, foxes, and house cats — keeping them focused on the tip of her tail and away from her vital parts. Both short- and long-tailed weasels have black-tipped tails, but least weasels, *Mustela nivalis*, the smallest of the North American weasels and the smallest member of the order Carnivora, do not. On a tail less than two inches long a black spot so close to the body would invite, rather than discourage, a fatal encounter with a predator.

A week later, on October 21, Weas was as white as snow. Of course there was no snow in October, and far from being camouflaged, she stood out like neon. But by mid-November the snow caught up with her, and her liquid movements became more shadowy and less obvious. Judging from the museum skins I have examined and reports I have heard, short-tailed weasels in northern New England take three weeks to complete their autumn molt and do so, at least in the Connecticut River Valley, from late September to late November. From an evolutionary standpoint this variation in timing makes perfect sense: since fewer white weasels are caught by predators on snowy terrain, early snows favor those weasels who molt early. When snows are late, those who molt in November are favored. It's called hedging your bets. Washed in night light, Weas was luminescent. Linny and I set up lawn chairs on the outside of her pen and watched her beneath all phases of the moon, beneath a thin curtain of northern lights, and on those velvet nights when the moon is late. Friends joined us for viewing parties, sitting in the pen Indian-style or gathered on the outside, eating barbecued food while Weas patrolled the stonewall.

On the Sunday before Thanksgiving Day we hosted a Montshire fund raiser called "Weasel and Waffles." A total of sixty-seven people came for breakfast and to see Weas scoot through the stonewall. They arrived in small groups at half-hour intervals.

"How many weasels do you have?"

I answered that question at least once every half hour, for Weas moved in and out of opposite ends of the stonewall so fast and so often that few would have disputed my claim if I had announced that a pair made their home in the pen. Some might even have believed three. Preschoolers sang rounds of "Pop Goes the Weasel," and for older kids we unraveled her role in the web of life by comparing Weas to a disease-fighting white blood cell.

"Who knows what part of our body fights disease?" I'd ask.

Someone would reply, "White blood cells."

"Well, then, do you know that the forest is like a great shaggy body that suffers from disease? One illness that plagues the forest is the "too-many" disease: too many mice, too many squirrels, too many chipmunks. Nature has agents like white blood cells to fight this disease." Here I'd pause, then ask "And who is one of the white blood cells of the forest?"

Watching Weas move about for prolonged minutes was a privilege few of the waffle crowd, or anyone else for that matter, had enjoyed for longer than a glimpse in the wild. Once, on a trip near the mouth of the Knife River by the edge of Hudson Bay, a short-tailed weasel entertained a museum party of seventeen for most of an afternoon, darting from its security under our cottage steps to accept flakes of dried fish. And once, when Linny hiked the Norwegian tundra, a short-tailed weasel called a "stoat" by the British came out from an overhang of roots along the trail to watch her urinate. Other than occurrences like those, all of our wild weasel sightings were quick. I've squeaked, mouselike, to call them out of stonewalls and watched as they bounded away through white woods. And late one winter night an ermine crossed in front of our car and ran into a field of stubble corn lit by a gibbous moon. Now whenever Linny and I pass that spot we slow down, half expecting the ermine to reappear.

When the snows came Weas' pen filled up, softening the contours of her domain and covering the stonewall. She burrowed through the drifts, half swimming half running. Neat round holes peppered the surface, and as the temperature dropped the snow froze, so she kept to her network of subnivian tunnels, appearing only at one hole or another to accept food. If I released a deer mouse down one of the tunnels, Weas moved in for the kill beneath the mantle of ice and snow, tracking the mouse by scent and sound. Once I listened, ear to the ice, to her muffled screams as she pursued a meadow vole more than two feet below me.

By January I began to go for days without seeing Weas. She chiseled frozen meat from the DORs that I tossed into her pen and quenched her enormous thirst with snow and chips of ice at night. Her tiny footprints told me she moved more by night than by day. By the end of March, when the snow had melted, I cleaned a graveyard of bones and hides and feathers from the pen. As I piled up the relics of her winter banquets, Weas emerged chirping from the stonewall. Her face was spotted with brown above the eyes and around the whiskers like the waning fields of snow. So was her tail. And a brown streak followed the curve of her spine from the rump midway up the back, then faded down her white sides.

I kept Weas for another spring and summer. She turned white eight days earlier the following autumn. By early November snow whitened the pen, and she caught scents on the cold night currents. I began feeding her large DORs, ruffed grouse and gray squirrels, and young white laboratory rats, pink-eyed albinos that Dartmouth College had generously supplied. She scattered her food below the snow and throughout the pen, on either side of the wall, and against the hardware cloth. Every third day I gave her a rat that she quickly disposed of, white on white against the snow. One evening in early December, as I hurried to keep an appointment, I tossed the last of the young rats into the pen and left without watching the coup de grâce. For the following two weeks I gave Weas DORs, an occasional deer mouse which she killed in her usual fashion, and balls of chopped meat. Then the big snows came and I began leaving her dinner by the door. In the morning it was always gone.

After not having seen Weas for six days, I entered the pen one morning and rattled the stonewall. No response. I rattled longer and louder, and still no response. I dug the snow away from the base of the wall, rattling the stones once more. A white face poked out, but it was not the face of a weasel. It was a sharp face with ruby eyes, a rat face. The last rat I had tossed into the pen had somehow survived and grown up, drinking Weas' water, eating her food, and when it had reached sufficent size, five or six times heavier and several inches longer than a female short-tailed weasel, it killed and ate Weas. I tore apart the stonewall, stomped on the rat as it tried to escape, then grabbed it by the tail and beat it repeatedly against a rock.

I built Weas her home, toted her water, and hauled her food. She was my iridescent window to a special wilderness. I had become her captive.

6

SOURCES

MY GRANDMOTHER WHEELED ME THROUGH the labyrinthine halls of New York's American Museum of Natural History, past a herd of mounted Indian elephants, a herd of African elephants, beneath the life-size model of a blue whale hanging from the ceiling in the Hall of Marine Life, past the articulated bones of Mesozoic monsters — Allosaur, Stegosaur, Tyrannosaur — past endless lines of brass handrails just high enough for a two-year-old's fingers to slide on. Later, as I grew older, I focused on the innumerable life-size, lifelike dioramas in the North American habitat groups:

> Midnight on Gunflint Lake, north lies Ontario. December. The temperature's fallen well below zero. The aurora borealis shimmers — blue and green and red. The Big Dipper. A great gray owl in a birch; lines of black spruce scratch the horizon. Deer tracks spot the snow, close together in a walk at first then farther apart in a run. Two timber wolves — the main theme — frozen in midstride have set the deer in motion. Midnight, northern Minnesota, Gunflint Lake.

The glass partitions to the dioramas were windows into the wilderness. Beyond each pane was an exact habitat — a sliver of primitive North America — replete with synthetic leaves and flowers, rocks and fallen logs, snags, ledges, riverine ice, and whatever else was congruous with the geography of the place exhibited. Later, as my natural-history skills improved, I would challenge myself to identify the vegetation and the incidental animals that complemented the main theme, checking my answers against the key that accompanied each diorama.

The backgrounds, meticulously painted scenes impregnated with a sense of time, place, and motion, curved around and blended with an often sprawling foreground. They were no less than mural art. The finest natural-history artists of the first half of the twentieth century — Carl Rungus, Francis Lee Jaques, and Louis Agassiz Fuertes, among others — contributed to the splendor of the North American habitat groups. The more I traveled around the country the more I realized that the murals were not just composite habitats but were precise geographic renderings: the north shore of Lake Umbagog in Maine, the Merced River in Yosemite, Wildcat Mountain in New Hampshire, the Delaware Water Gap. In each of the background murals I eventually recognized specific skylines, river bends, and waterfalls. Later, in the shadow of Mount Sunapee, I was to sit by the very bend of a little rocky stream whose exact likeness had been rendered in the Hall of North American Forests.

The taxidermy in the dioramas was exquisite. As a child I expected the animals — two bull moose dueling on the Alaskan tundra, their muscles rippling like waves — to flinch. As I got older I wondered why the big mounts didn't fall over or how the bald eagle was suspended in the air. That overall sense of place and time, that dynamic sense of drama, that sense of being out there, alone and watching, like an Indian or a John James Audubon or a John Bachman, was mystical and for me always kept "The Museum" one step beyond "The Zoo."

A couple of dioramas were eulogies to extinction — a flock of Carolina parakeets in a southeastern forest, a Labrador duck on a snow-covered rock off Montauk Point, Long Island. Another, Late

August in Hackensack Meadows, in northern New Jersey, with its flocks of bobolinks and tree swallows, has become an inadvertent eulogy to a habitat that has been crippled by industrial pollution and the Meadowlands sports complex. And the tree line in Quebec's Chic-Chocs, with its lynx and snowshoe hare and distant woodland caribou, looks like the White Mountains except that both lynx and caribou no longer cross the border.

> Late afternoon, north slope of Mount Albert. Northwest lies the St. Lawrence River, northeast the Table Mountains. End of October. Snow glazes the highlands. Gray sky, bands of blue. A line of sunset orange. Two ravens overhead; six woodland caribou, all antlered, and an apron of evergreen. Snowshoe hare cowering beneath a twisted fir. A lynx — the main theme — pads closer. Late afternoon, Gaspe Peninsula, Mount Albert.

Going to the American Museum of Natural History was better than watching television, even better that Walt Disney's "True Life Adventures." The museum was a citadel for my itinerant imagination, a great treasure chest of information with exhibits beautiful, profound, and thrilling. Science and art merged into an inseparable whole. When I see a fisher I see more than just a quick, grizzled-brown mustelid with a taste for porcupines. I see a link in the million-year-old chain of fisher evolution. I see a distillate of the Green Mountains, a collection of complex adaptations shaped by local environmental forces that have combed through the genes of unnumbered generations to select this functional, this successful, this beautiful design — the fisher.

For a would-be naturalist, books from the museum's retail shop were like gifts from the gods, and with them I brought the dioramas home. My first copy of *Mammals: A Golden Nature Guide* was an instant hit, a third-grade bible, and I wore it out memorizing its pictures and words. Each biography in the pocket-sized book was distilled to its essence, which for an eight-year-old was a cornucopia of facts. I learned that the lynx, the bobtailed cat of the north, is a shy creature of the night, and that despite their respective reputations, woodchucks don't forecast the weather and flying squirrels don't fly. There is fear and loathing, I discovered, in wolverine

country, and everywhere populations of snowshoe hare rise and fall like ocean tides. Red foxes come in four colors, all with white-tipped tails. California sea lions perform in the circus; coyotes cooperate; and jaguars, on occasion, ford the Rio Grande River into Texas.

I have been building upon these and like facts ever since and have come to realize that I've been imprinted by the color illustrations that accompanied the *Golden Nature Guide's* descriptions. Coyotes, for instance, should look like emaciated German shepherds and hump-backed whales should always smile. Those simplistic renderings, unlike the detailed and cryptic scene of a Robert Bateman painting, framed the mammal within a narrowly defined habitat. And like bubbles, many of those scenes — the sea otter, for instance, floating in a kelp bed or the herd of bison in front of a prairie fire — still rise vividly to the surface of my mind whenever I encounter the animal in question in the wild. When I think of pine martens I see a marten on a horizontal limb, its head turned toward the right to show its burnt-orange throat. Over the marten's rump is a sprig of white pine and a warbler; below and behind, across the entire page, is the blue-green of boreal Maine. While hiking the Vogelsang Trail in Yosemite National Park in 1971, a pine marten bolted from a jumble of boulders and ran across my foot. When I regained my composure, I felt somehow cheated. Martens belonged with conifers and red squirrels, not pikas and alpine meadows. Had I been able to articulate my inchoate needs, I would have ordered my marten on a pine limb, looking east, the blue haze of Maine in the background.

Because of that little book I associate opossums with persimmons, striped skunks with tin cans, kit foxes with abandoned pueblos, mountain lions with rim rock, muskrats with cattails, buck white-tailed deer with autumn ponds. And when I think of the ideal fisher scene — it's not in my bathroom — it's on a pine limb against a background of pointed spruce, a beautiful blue lake and the snow-capped crown of Mount Hood, or Mount Shasta, or Mount Olympus.

In the museum's old Hall of Reptiles and Amphibians I got reacquainted with red-backed salamanders, the tiny occupants of North

Wantagh's greenbelt. These wormlike amphibians stimulated my intellectual curiosity. Apart from their Batesian mimicry, their indication of beech-maple woodlands, and their efficient use of energy, red-backed salamanders are on the cutting edge of salamander evolution. At the museum I learned that they are lungless salamanders of the family Plethodontidae, the most advanced salamanders in the world. Instead of lungs, red-backed salamanders breathe through their thin, moist skin and the lining of their throats, a novel arrangement among quadrupeds. Unlike Fowler's toads and garter snakes — the other vertebrates of my youth — these salamanders caught my interest more by what I read than by what I saw. And the books I bought from the museum shop offered more grist for my mill.

I first read Karl Kauffeld's *Snakes and Snake Hunting* more than twenty-five years ago. Here was the story of a grown man who tramped about, a sack and forked stick in hand, collecting snakes for the Staten Island Zoo. He waded through the swamps of South Carolina, poked around the mesas of Arizona, and climbed the talus slopes of southern New York state. For me, *Snakes and Snake Hunting* was a revelation. I discovered that baseball players were not the only adults engaged in the sport of children. Kauffeld roamed throughout North America foraging for snakes wherever the air was sweet, the sky blue. And he was paid for his travels and for his memoirs. One chapter had a lasting effect on me. "The Denizens of Dutchess" recounted Kauffeld's adventures with timber rattlesnakes and copperheads in New York's Taconic Mountains. What amazed me then (and still does) is that these maligned snakes lived so close to New York City. Within two and a half hours of my neighborhood were the ancient hibernacula of venomous snakes. Not only Dutchess but Putnam and Westchester counties harbored the fabled serpents. They lived right at the back door of the City.

These snakes were not the scourge of the Northeast; they were animals of great myth and misinformation. Had they legs, they would have run with deer; had they voices, they would have wailed with loons. Copperheads and timber rattlesnakes, masterpieces shaped by local environmental forces acting by natural selection, are designed to follow the infrared trails of small mammals over the rocks and soil of deciduous woods. Unfortunately, when I reached Dover Plains in Dutchess County many years later, rattlesnakes were rare. I wasn't the only boy to have read Kauffeld's book. Over-zealous naturalists, both amateur and professional, gathered up the dark-colored rattlers for exhibitions and private collections. Karl Kauffeld's enthusiasm and geographic descriptions were much too inspiring.

After I finished college the museum continued to be an incomparable resource. I often went behind the scenes to the curatorial offices to beg answers from the scientists working there. When I had a problem recognizing winter-plumage golden plovers from black-bellies, John Bull of the Department of Ornithology set me up among the cabinets of shorebird study skins. When I needed hair samples from native northern New England mammals to help me identify the prey remains in fisher, the Department of Mammalogy gave me a pair of tweezers and a map to the cabinets of mammal skins. And before I left for South America in 1983, it was at the museum that I got my first introduction to neotropical jungle birds.

The American Museum of Natural History has never stopped surprising me. Checking black-bellied plover skins, collected after the birds had left their circumpolar breeding grounds, was my first vivid glimpse at how small and fragile our planet really is. From the data cards that accompany the skins I learned that they touched down on the coastlines of every continent except Antarctica and almost all the major archipelagos and islands — China, India, Columbia, Brazil, Somaliland, Borneo, Queensland, Hawaii, Japan, Siberia, Long Island. Here was a truly cosmopolitan bird that regularly transgressed the world's biogeographical and political boundaries. Among a drawerful of short-tailed weasel skins, I found a ratty specimen collected by Theodore Roosevelt on January 18, 1874, in Barnard, Maine. In the next cabinet, I found a long-tailed weasel from Sunapee, New Hampshire, collected on February 1, 1937, by Clarence Hay, the father of writer and naturalist John Hay. Down the hall, among thousands of other deer mice skins, I picked up one that was trapped and stuffed by Ernest Thompson Seton.

One of my biggest surprises at the museum was very much alive and riding the employees' elevator. As I leaned patiently against a chrome handrail, waiting to reach the fifth-floor curatorial offices, a shy graduate student afraid to make eye-contact with the luminaries, the stem of a hand-carved cane caught my attention. Slowly my eyes climbed the cane, traveled over twisted, convoluted figurines decorated by a culture light-years from my own, and rested on a small weathered hand. From hand, to baggy sweater, to a shoulder inches below my own, my eyes traveled. When I glanced at the old woman's face, I was startled to recognize Margaret Mead.

7

TIMBER RATTLESNAKE:
ENDANGERED AND UNLOVED

A FRIEND GAVE ME A MILK SNAKE during my junior year in college. He had found it coiled beneath a tractor tire on a western Louisiana farm close to the Sabine River. I named the snake Bowie and kept him for more than a year. He entertained my friends, for he tolerated handling and never bit anything larger than laboratory mice, five-lined skinks, or fledgling English sparrows. Bowie crawled through hands and around wrists, and, unless restrained, continued up under shirts to coil in the dark warmth of upper arms. Whenever biceps flexed, his grip gently tightened like a blood-pressure cuff.

Bowie and I had several housemates at Ball State University. One of these had a girl friend with a two-year-old daughter, Nicole, who was drawn to the milk snake. For Nicole, Bowie was a multi-colored toy banded in black and yellow and blotched with red. Gentle and unassuming, he grazed her with his dark forked tongue and she broadcasted exuberance. One evening when I was away, Nicole left the terrarium lid open, and Bowie escaped. Several days later, after a grueling bout in the organic-chemistry lab, I pulled up our driveway to find four neighborhood boys marching across the lawn, a limp milk snake in the crotch of their forked stick. Like pagans, they chanted and glorified their deed as, watching, I felt sick to my stomach.

In the summer of 1972 I made my first visit to Walden Pond. (Technically speaking, Walden is not a pond but a lake, because its large, deep waters stratify each summer according to their temperature and density.) Along the hiking trail that circles the pond and not far from the jumble of stones that marks the site of Thoreau's cabin there was the sound of a commotion, then the sound of a gunshot. As I rounded a corner I saw a hefty ranger, pistol in hand, directing hikers around a mortally wounded milk snake. The man was clearly proud of himself, as though he had rid Massachusetts of a great evil, and gloated like a tackle who had just recovered a fumble. "Damned copperheads, they'll make you sicker than a dog," he announced. Before the crowd dispersed I grabbed the milk snake, pointed out its distinguishing features, and referred the ranger to several reptile field guides. His face tightened and reddened, not the deep red of a red-belly snake, but rather a lighter shade of human humiliation, more like the pink flush in the eye of a northern water snake.

Like northeastern milk snakes, copperheads are tan, but the similarity ends there. Their heads are broad and triangular, their pupils elliptical. Their bodies are thick and are banded with deep brown hourglasses. Altogether, copperheads are more masculine and more threatening looking (although hardly more aggressive), than slender, inoffensive milk snakes. This problem of mistaken identity between copperheads and milk snakes works both ways. Later that same summer a message reached my office in the Education Department of the Bronx Zoo that a youth with a brown paper bag full of young copperheads was hawking snakes for fifty cents apiece in the Crotona Parking Lot. Fortunately, no one was bitten. Neither the young entrepreneur nor his customers knew what they had gotten their hands into.

In 1974 I was employed at Cumberland Gap National Historic Site, the token naturalist among a staff of history buffs. While in eastern Kentucky I met two types of snake people: those who hated snakes and killed them quickly, and those who hated snakes and killed them more slowly. Some collected them for Baptist Church meetings to express their faith by fondling them before God and the congregation. Both types worked for the National Park Service. One afternoon I followed a ranger, a lanky, balding, tobacco-chewing man from over the mountain, who, if he hadn't been hired to enforce the law and protect our natural heritage, would probably have worked in the coal mines and bootlegged whiskey. As we drove up Pinnacle Road a timber rattlesnake eased onto the warm pavement to soak up the last of the day's heat. He slowed down, leaned out of the car door, and *bang* — with a single shot he slew the serpent, then slammed the door and drove away.

During its 1979 legislative session, the state of New Hampshire passed a comprehensive bill to protect endangered and threatened vertebrates whose ranges included all or part of the state. I was among a team of naturalists invited to the Harris Center in Hancock to recommend to the commissioner of fish and game which animals warranted inclusion on the state's new endangered species list. After six hours of debating the relative merits of the more than forty animals proposed for the list, we voted, using a point system devised by New York State that assigned numbers to various wildlife categories according to their degree of rarity, and their scientific and scenic value. The system was designed to determine which animals needed the most help, a form of triage on the battlefield of beleaguered species.

Timber rattlesnakes received a rating of 25, two points higher than the arbitrary cut-off for threatened species and only .6 of a point lower than the rating given to peregrine falcons, the recipients of a multimillion-dollar, nationwide restoration effort. Except for peregrines and Atlantic salmon — another distinguished creature in the conservation limelight — timber rattlesnakes had the third highest ranking, higher than bald eagles, osprey, and loons, even higher than lynx — which were on the verge on extinction — and pine marten, which were already gone. But at the insistence of Fish and Game Commissioner Charles Berry, and to the chagrin of few, rattlesnakes were axed from the official endangered species list submitted to the governor.

I have never seen a New England timber rattlesnake. I would consider such an encounter on a par with seeing a bald eagle or a lynx. Each year the chances are greater that I won't see one, for rattlesnakes are gone from Maine and are disappearing fast from Vermont and New Hampshire before word can spread about their unique and specialized accommodations to the ledges, the woods, and the weather. The Northeast was theirs for hundreds of thousands of years, perhaps longer. Few people care that timber rattlesnakes are dying out. And few conservation groups will risk offending their members with a declaration of concern for them, northern New England's only venomous snakes.

So deep runs the fear of rattlesnakes in Vermont that the Fair Haven town clerk refused my telephone request to discuss the town's old rattlesnake bounty records, reacting as though the book was cursed. And across the Connecticut River, in Bear Brook State Park near Concord, where all plants and animals are protected by the state, timber rattlesnakes are mysteriously killed. Henry Laramie, a retired state biologist, refuses to divulge the location of live snakes because of his concern about the snakes' attrition rate. Every spring he surveys Bear Brook and finds fewer rattlesnakes. It is easy to mobilize concern for whales and wolves, sea otters and condors, or any game animal, but when the topic turns to timber rattlesnakes concern falls on deaf ears.

Historically, timber rattlesnakes ranged from southern Maine through the southern Appalachians, westward to Wisconsin, eastern Kansas, and Oklahoma, southward to the Mississippi Valley and eastward to Texas. They were the first venomous snake encountered by the Pilgrims, the first New World snake classified by Carolus Linnaeus. Unlike turkeys and cranberries, timber rattlesnakes were not embraced by the colonists. By 1744 they were already rare near Philadelphia, wrote William Bartram. And when Linnaeus conferred the seemingly opprobrious scientific name *Crotalus horridus* upon them, all but Latin scholars assumed the snake was named for its evil ways. Although the roots are the same, the Latin *horridus* has nothing to do with horrid or horrible: it means "rough," "bristling," "scaly," and is a somewhat veiled reference to the texture of the snake's skin, for all rattlesnakes have keeled scales — a thin median ridge projecting from each scale. *Crotalus* — the largest of the two genera of rattlesnakes — is from the Greek *crotala*, which means "castanet" or "musical rattle," a fitting epithet.

Their name aside, timber rattlesnakes inherited the wrath of the snake-terrorized world. In 1842 Zadoc Thompson wrote that they were nearly gone from Vermont, and just a century ago fewer than two thousand crept among ledges in all of northern New England. Far fewer creep there today. To the Hopi, rattlesnakes are symbols of fertility. To them, water represents life and growth, and rattlesnakes, whose singing tails mimic the sound of rain against the hard-packed desert floor, are a sign from the spirit world that rain is forthcoming. Our own view of rattlesnakes is more venomous than the snakes themselves. All the fear and loathing timber rattlesnakes evoke in people is undeserved. They are timid snakes. In the recorded history of Vermont only a single fatal snakebite is reported: a weathered tombstone in Putney reads, "Killed by a Serpente." In North America more people die from lightning bolts and bee stings or in their bathtubs than from the fangs of venomous reptiles. Worldwide, about one or two people out of every ten million succumb to snakebite.

Rattlesnakes belong to the subfamily Crotalinae of the family Viperidae, the most advanced family of reptiles in the world. On the high plains of North America, at the dawn of the Pliocene epoch between four and twelve million years ago, rattlesnakes differentiated from their more generally adapted viperid ancestors, leaving their fossils — mostly vertebrae with occasional ribs, fangs and skull bones — in gypsum and limestone caves and in the asphalt pits of California. During the first wave of rattlesnake evolution the interior grasslands were crowded with ancient horses, camels, and numerous species of bison and pronghorn antelope that moved together in rivers across the prairie. Most viperids and many species of nonpoisonous snakes vibrate the tips of their tails to produce a rattle against dry leaves in order to avoid being stepped on. Rattlesnakes, which evolved amid all those cloven hooves, developed resonators on the end of their tails to amplify the vibratory noise. Only two species of North

American crotalids lack rattles: the water moccasin and the copperhead. Both dwell in areas that lack large populations of ungulates: moccasins prefer swamps, and copperheads inhabit rocky outcrops and deep woods.

Of the thirty-one species of rattlesnakes, all are confined to the New World. Fifteen are in the United States (four east of the Mississippi River) and the rest inhabit the deserts and humid forests of Central and South America. Twenty-eight species belong to *Crotalus*, the mailed rattlesnakes, the most recently evolved genus. Each has numerous small scales (as well as a few large ones) on the top of the head suggesting the small overlapping rings or loops of chain mail armor. The remaining three species, in the genus *Sistrurus* — including the pygmy rattler of the Southeast and the massasauga of the Midwest and the lake states — sport nine large skull plates instead of the tiny scales.

With the exception of the western rattlesnake, the timber rattlesnake has the most extensive range of any rattlesnake species in North America. Until recently two subspecies were recognized: the timber rattlesnake, *C. h. horridus*, of the Appalachian highlands and northern deciduous forests, and the canebrake rattlesnake, *C. h. atricaudatus*, of the swampy southern coastal plain and the Mississippi Valley. Now both are considered a single race of the same species. Throughout their range timber rattlesnakes reach lengths of four to six feet and sometimes longer in the rich, warm swampland of the Southeast.

During spring and fall timber rattlesnakes are diurnal, retreating at night down into their hibernacula. In the heat of the summer sun they leave their hibernacula and reverse the pattern: By day they rest in the shade of overhanging ledges or on the shadowed side of fallen trees and stumps. At night they hunt, emerging at sundown to follow the infrared trails of their warm-blooded prey, small mammals and ground-nesting birds. All crotalids have two heat-sensitive facial pits — one on each side of the head between the eye and the nostril — which are more prominent than the nostrils, giving rise to their collective common name, pit vipers. So sensitive are these facial pits to the infrared rays and body heat shed by small mammals that a blindfolded timber rattlesnake can accurately locate and strike a mouse, distinguishing less than a one-degree difference between its own body temperature and that of its prey.

Once it locates its prey the snake approaches within striking distance — about half its body length — then coils up and strikes. Its fangs are hollow and movable, and when not in use they fold back against the roof of the mouth. Each fang moves independently and is controlled voluntarily by the snake. Venom is squeezed from the rattlesnake's parotid glands, on the roof of the mouth behind the eyes, through a pair of venom ducts that plug into the fangs. It is released as the fangs contact the prey. Viperids are the only poisonous snakes with movable hypodermiclike fangs. Cobras and coral snakes, by contrast, have grooved and fixed front fangs, and rear-fanged snakes like the African boomslang must grab their prey and chew before the venom reaches the wound. In poisonous snakes the parotid glands produce a complex and modified saliva. Once injected, venom from a timber rattlesnake snake not only kills but also begins to digest the prey by dissolving its blood vessels. A keeper and I once offered a laboratory mouse to a young copperhead that was off-exhibit at the Bronx Zoo. After it was bitten we removed the unfortunate mouse and dissected it. Within five minutes its body cavity had become soupy, thick, and brick-colored as the organs and vessels began to leak. If we had allowed the mouse to flee and extended the same courtesy to the copperhead, the snake, using its facial pits, would have followed the mouse's warm trail like a bloodhound.

Of all of northern New England's snakes (which is only eleven species), timber rattlers have the shortest season of activity. They are the last to emerge from hibernation and the first to withdraw in the fall. By May 10 most rattlers have left their ancestral hibernacula below the frost line among the jumbled boulders of south-facing slopes. For a few weeks they loiter on the ledges soaking up spring sunshine and retreating below the surface at night when the temperature drops. Soon after they emerge from hibernation, timber rattlers convene to breed. When night temperatures rise to a comfortable level the breeding season ends, and the snakes leave the ledges for the wooded valleys.

By late August females return to the neighborhood of the hibernacula to give birth. A few weeks later all of the snakes gather to await the frost. As the nights grow progressively longer and colder, they stop crawling to the surface of the ledges to catch the sun and remain below the frost line at the base of deep — sometimes twenty or more feet — vertical fissures. Hibernation begins. Eight months later timber rattlesnakes emerge again from their winter dormitory.

Hundreds of rattlesnakes once shared the same hibernaculum. When I visited the Dutchess County dens made famous by Karl Kauffeld's book, I was astonished to find the entrances worn smooth by the abrasive action of belly scales. So many snakes for so many years had collectively scoured the rock with the force of a small glacier. Now the snakes have been reduced to a handful per site. The old bounty system and the fear of rattlesnakes brought people to the ledges with rifles, axes, and clubs. It is a wonder that any snakes survive today. Although records exist for timber rattlesnakes in Freeport and Central Islip, by the turn of the twentieth century the only rattlesnakes on Long Island hung as trophies in old farmhouses. In Rhode Island they are restricted to one locality and will surely pass from the state. In Pennsylvania roundups no longer draw a big crowd, for rattlesnakes are increasingly harder to find. The use of snake oil as a panacea lead to their extermination before 1920 on Rattlesnake Island in Lake Winnipesaukee, New Hampshire's largest lake.

Timber rattlesnakes are now doomed in the Northeast for other reasons. Normally yellow, brown, or gray, with unmarked heads and dark blotches in front forming crossbands on the rear, some northern rattlesnakes are almost black. These melanistic specimens, mostly males, bring a high price on the live-snake market and are coveted by snake fanciers for their menageries, both professional and private. Many historic sites have been worked so often by collectors that the hibernacula are now empty. With each succeeding year fewer and fewer timber rattlesnakes leave the ledges for the wooded valleys. Massachusetts and Rhode Island have passed legislation to protect the snakes and their hibernacula. Mount Tom in Massachusetts' Holyoke Range even has a snake warden sponsored by the state and the Massachusetts Audubon Society. Not much is happening in New

Hampshire, but in Vermont the Nature Conservancy conducted field surveys of the known hibernacula and plans to purchase several critical sites. It may be too late.

I visited the Fair Haven town clerk last summer to examine the town's old rattlesnake bounty records. "Why," she asked, "would anyone care?" That was a hard question to answer. I had just driven an hour and a half to learn something about the snakes and about the people of western Vermont, maybe something about the limestone ledges. I found it difficult to articulate what it was I was after. She pressed me again.

"It's not every day someone comes here to talk about snakes. I don't even know where *that* book is."

She apparently found it hard to say the word, *rattlesnake*.

"I saw one this spring, crossing the road. I can't stand to look at 'em," she said.

A man in a three-piece suit walked into the office. He was in a hurry.

"Hey Bob," the clerk snapped, "this guy wants to know about raaattttlesnakes." Finally she had said the word, hanging onto the *a*'s and *t*'s as though she were shaking a castanet. Until that moment I hadn't thought of the word "rattle" or "rattlesnake" onomatopoetically. Already I had learned something.

Bob didn't like snakes either. He had killed a timber rattlesnake in West Castleton, not far from Lake Bomoseen, a couple of years previously. Whacked its head off with a hoe, he said. He swelled with pride as he recounted the deed. Both Bob and the town clerk agreed that I looked like a snake and therefore was up to no good.

No one wanted to touch the bounty book, so I got it myself. This is what I found: Between 1899 and 1904, 241 timber rattlesnakes were bountied. The earliest bounty was paid on May 9, the latest on October 19. Of those 241 rattlesnakes, 62 were killed between May 9 and May 31, and 154 after August 21. In terms of their natural history, this confirmed that timber rattlesnakes go to bed early and wake up late. It is no wonder that here, at the northern edge of their range, with only five-and-a-half months to feed and grow, timber rattlesnakes breed every other year and do not reach sexual maturity until their fifth or sixth year.

Two-and-a-half times as many snakes were killed in fall than in spring. Considering their natural history this, too, makes sense. Since timber rattlesnakes are communal hibernators, they breed in May when the gangs are still all together. In mid-August the females return to the ancestral hibernacula to bear young. After the births, the local population peaks in August and September. One snake hunter, Andy Howard, collected the one-dollar bounty on 196 rattlesnakes during that five-year period. According to the town clerk, Andy liked his liquor and the bounty payments warmed the long, cold Vermont winters. Andy had made it his business to find the snakes' hibernacula. On September 13, 1902, he killed 37 rattlesnakes. Only 25 snakes were bountied between early June and mid-August. Again, this is not too surprising. Like tomatoes and corn, timber rattlesnakes are ready to grow only after the last frost and leave the hibernacula for the wooded valleys — often traveling miles from their ledges — to hunt mice and squirrels and cottontails. To find one in the summer is a matter of chance. There were no records from 1905 through 1947. After 1947, 64 snakes were killed within a twenty-year period ending in 1967. With so few snakes to record, the bounty book began noting the length and number of rattles of each snake: the longest snake was four-and-a-half feet, most were three to three-and-a half feet. One brave woman killed one that had eleven rattles. Since the dollar bounty hadn't changed, either the price of booze had risen or the timber rattlesnake population had plummeted. I feared the latter.

I left the Fair Haven town clerk's office, driving north on Route 22A to see the snake ledges. The scene was more like Tennessee or Kentucky than Vermont. The land was flat and wooded, rising abruptly into a series of limestone escarpments that paralleled the road. Except for a few red and chestnut oaks and some bright graffiti, the ledges were bare, white and gleaming in the afternoon sun. Old and wrinkled, they faced southwest. I pulled into a parking lot off Route 22A and asked the proprietor of a hunting and fishing shop about rattlesnakes. He hated them too. A month before, he told me, a couple of teenagers climbed up to the ledges and bludgeoned a young snake. And just the week before, his neighbor had killed another in his backyard. I explained that timber rattlesnakes are a valuable cog in the wheel that dampens the ever-expanding rodent population, that they are the most threatened vertebrate in northern New England, and that they are found in fewer than a dozen sites in Vermont and New Hampshire. "Good," he retorted. "Damn those goddamn snakes, I don't give a damn if they're endangered. I'll kill 'em whenever I see 'em. Law or no law."

In response to a column I subsequently wrote about the snakes, I received a letter a week later from a ninety-four-year-old Windsor man named John E. Rockstrom. He told his own story about timber rattlesnakes.

> I was born in Norwood, Massachusetts and the oldest of four children, three boys and one girl. We lived in a double-family farmhouse where the farm had been abandoned and now was part of the village area of the town. I spent a lot of time in the nearby woods, and of course saw various types of small animal life and birds. . . . Once I was picking lowbush blueberries in the woods in back of our house and . . . there was a sharp buzzing sound and something hit the end of my middle finger real hard. I jumped back real quick and an open wound and a little blood was there. My finger was swelling and I was scared. . . . When mother saw the wound she ran to the folks at the other end of the house, who somehow got word to the doctor who came in a horse-drawn buggy. When he heard my story as he was examining my finger, he said "young man, you have been bit by a rattlesnake . . ." I was sick for quite a while. None of us ever went near that blueberry patch again. Below the blueberry patch was a swamp called "Snake Up." I had heard about milk snakes and large black "bull" snakes [black racers], and we young ones were never to stone them but to go away and leave them alone because they did no harm.

This is the only person I have ever heard from who actually was bitten by a timber rattlesnake, and yet he respected the animal. A few years after his bite, Mr. Rockstrom recalled, he was gathering nuts in the Blue Hills near Readville, Massachusetts. There were rattlers there, too.

We would . . . thrash the grass and many times we disturbed young rattlers, then we would leave the chestnuts alone for a spell. [Then] we would pick loads of them.

Now here is a man who suffered a snake bite and still recognizes the value of milk snakes and black racers. And best of all, nowhere in his long letter did he advocate the destruction of timber rattlesnakes, only avoidance. Maybe I should forward John Rockstrom's remarks and stories to the town clerk in Fair Haven. On second thought, she'd probably dismiss the letter as the work of a serpent.

8

THE COMING OF
THE EASTERN COYOTE

THROUGHOUT THE NIGHT they sent their voices toward the December moon and its attendant clouds. Wild, wondrous paeans were hurled to the heavens, coyotes answering echoes, echoes answering coyotes, then sent back to the rolling hills again before fading away. I had heard them sing before in the deserts of Arizona and the mountains of California, on the staked plains and in the dust of west Texas, but this was different. This was on the bank of the Connecticut River and these beleaguered minstrels were eastern coyotes howling from the shadow of a sugarbush and an old stonewall.

I admire eastern coyotes. Most Yankees don't. From the instant their hollow voices rose above a whisper, hunters have blamed them for the natural oscillation of game animals. Coyotes are blamed for competing for ruffed grouse and snowshoe hare in particular, for gray squirrels, and for cottontails in southern New England, as well as for a decline in the deer herd. Most sheep farmers, livid with rage when the conversation turns to coyotes, advocate a second coming of the bounty system. Although they feed mainly on small mammals, carrion, and some vegetation — not mutton or venison — eastern coyotes stir a hatred so great, so injudicious, that they face another Inquisition.

Gene Letourneau, a syndicated "catch 'em and cook 'em" columnist from Maine and a woodsman old enough to know better, wrote a condemning exposé on eastern coyotes, entitled *America's New Wolf*. For the cover Letourneau chose a circular photograph of a catatonic coyote gripped in a leg-hold trap, implying a view through the scope of a high-powered rifle. Only the cross hairs are missing. In the rest of the book coyotes are pictured dead: stacked in the snow, strapped to jeeps, slung over the shoulders of grizzled woodsmen, or displayed by proud, bare-chested youths. According to Letourneau, eastern coyotes are a blemish on the fair face of New England, animals worthy of annihilation — certainly not celebration — because they threaten deer and sheep, perhaps even people.

"How Dangerous to People," the most twisted chapter in Letourneau's book, begins with the story of Hazen Hall — farmer, woodsman, marksman — from Amity, Maine. According to Letourneau, on August 25, 1981, as Hall thinned brush in his woodlot, four coyotes appeared in a clearing and fixed their ocher eyes on the woodcutter. As they advanced Hall was forced to the hood of his pickup where he busied the quartet with a chainsaw until he could grab his M1 rifle from inside the cab. One coyote was killed, the others fled. His pant leg ripped, his pride dashed, Hall reported the incident to a local wildlife commissioner who, Letourneau says, vouched for the man's credibility. Not everyone subscribed to Hazen Hall's story. One thing was certain, though. He did shoot a coyote, a four-month-old eighteen pounder with baby teeth, whose stomach, reported Peter Anderson of *The Boston Globe*, was packed with blueberries and chokecherries. That Hall could aim a rifle was not disputed either; three months after the spurious coyote attack Hall was tried for blowing his wife away.

Like a swarm of carrion flies, tall tales and black lies trail eastern coyotes from rural villages to the floors of state houses. At a 1977 legislative hearing, former New Hampshire state senator George

Wiggins — then a representative — told a credulous House committee that coyotes kill deer by the dozen, stacking their carcasses in the woods. He claimed personal experience in such matters, referring to the frozen deer as if they were neatly arranged deli salami. And the committee, which consisted mostly of sleepy octogenarians and hunters heeding misguided emotion rather than biologic fact, refused to recognize eastern coyotes as fur bearers (I'm not sure what they thought all that gray stuff sticking out of the animals' hides was), which would have elevated their status from varmint to that of a renewable resource. Instead of giving them a closed season the committee self-righteously recommended that the coyote season remain open all year.

During the late Pliocene epoch, two or three million years ago, the Rocky Mountains cast longer shadows on the plains, and the ancestors of modern mammals and birds grazed, crawled, flew, and loped across a virgin continent while the dawn coyote, *Canis lepophagus*, widespread and hungry, left his bones and those of his prey from Florida to the Pacific Coast. There was no one around to hate him then.

Indians reported first on coyotes. For the most part they liked what they saw, having left the animal an oral legacy and a name. For the Aztec of central Mexico he was *coyotl*, the barking dog. The Chinook of southwestern Washington and the Achomawl of California's Pit River Valley believed a coyote created the world from fog, sand, and sod. For the Ashochimi, Californians as well, a coyote appeared after the flood to plant feathers which sprouted, according to their colors, into several nations of people.

Coyotes also inherited the trickster role, being forever a tease and a proprietor of all that is odd, an animal with one foot in the Twilight Zone who nevertheless sits by the throne of the Great Spirit. Nothing is beyond the power of Coyote. The Maidu of California believe he used chicanery to defeat the Sun and fashion the night. And for the Crow of Montana, Coyote disguised his penis as a strawberry to lure a wife. To the southwestern Pueblo, coyotes, unable to subsist on such big game as desert bighorns, mule deer, or elk, are considered subordinate to wolves and mountain lions, both as predators and as animals. The Great Spirit, say the Pueblo, established rules for the hunt in which all predators had to fast for four days to provoke their hunger and leave a token from each kill for the Gods. But Coyote, always the opportunist and trickster, broke the proscription by killing and eating a jackrabbit without leaving an offering. After the hunt, the predators reassembled and the Great Spirit assured all but Coyote that game would be plentiful. For him, the Great Spirit decreed a scavenger's life of walking all day and all night. And because the coyote feeds on carrion, he became the Pueblo symbol of death. Unfortunately, we are deprived of Abenaki legends about coyotes, for the animals are Johnnies-come-lately to the Northeast.

On October 24, 1944, a fox hunter in Holderness, New Hampshire, shot a coyote, the first on record for New England. Four years later, one went down in Vermont. By 1957 coyotes reached Massachusetts and a year later, Connecticut. In 1983 an eastern coyote, coon fat on suburban garbage, arrived in Milton, only a few miles from downtown Boston. It was a healthy thirty-five pounds and accustomed to suburban living, noted *The Boston Globe*. After seeing coyotes for more than forty years in New England, however, people still call them "coydogs" — a fallacious reference to their pedigree — and blame them for everything but the weather. Along their path to the East, coyotes got tagged as hybrid dogs, a piece of misinformation that was spread by both the scientific and popular presses. But eastern coyotes, *Canis latrans variance*, a protean race evolving in the hills and woods of New England, are not mongrel dogs.

Their ancestors, a subspecies of the western coyote, *Canis latrans thamnos*, moved from the western bluestem prairies north and east into Ontario and Minnesota. By the turn of the century coyotes were established in the farming districts above Lakes Superior and Huron. Biologists speculate that a second wave of immigrants then contacted a small race of timber wolf in southern Ontario — the same race that had once howled in New England — whose fractured packs, having been dismantled by guns and poison, left them socially castrated. Lacking mates, lone wolves accepted coyotes. Before long the wolves vanished, absorbed into an expanding coyote population. This smidgen of wolf blood was sufficient, says Henry Hilton, who wrote a masters thesis on the subject, for Maine coyote skulls to average 11 percent wider and 6 percent longer than those of western coyotes. By the 1930s eastern coyotes arrived in New York again, on the heels of disappearing wolves. The rigid social order of wolves, which had kept their blood pure, had also kept coyotes west of the Great Lakes, running through brush country, prairies and deserts. But as gray wolves exited the Northeast and red wolves the Southeast, coyotes penetrated every state east of the Mississippi River, like pioneers in reverse.

Dogs, which are more or less genetically altered wolves, are not species-bound and readily mate with jackals, coyotes, wolves and dingoes, as well as with each other, a behavior that has given rise to their bewildering varieties. They also lack social allegiance. When dogs interbreed with coyotes (or anything else for that matter, including other dogs), males abandon the bitches with no regard for the puppies, and female dogs drive male coyotes away. Either way, the unsocial behavior of dogs toward their mates virtually guarantees the end of any "coydog" line. If by chance the hybrid pups survive, they face another formidable obstacle. Coydogs reach heat in November — months before eastern coyotes, thereby preventing any back-crossing — and give birth during the darkest, coldest time of the year when food is as scarce as sunlight. Coydogs behave like dogs. Eastern coyotes, on the other hand, conceive in late winter and give birth in spring when food supplies are replenished. Like wolves, male coyotes are dutiful fathers.

One late February morning along the Upper Ammonoosuc River in the wild, seldom-visited Kilkenny Range of the White Mountain National Forest, I picked up a female coyote's trail. Alone and in heat, she padded over the narrow frozen river, spotting the snow with urine and blood. Estrus blood was more than just a sign of passing, it was an invitation proclaiming her ripeness to any wayfaring male. Several weeks later, two coyotes moved along that same frozen stretch of river. From a plowed logging road, I saw that the female had company, for a larger set of coyote tracks had joined her own. No blood punctuated her trail, so I knew that she carried young. I stayed on the tracks, backtracking within a hundred yards of the river to where the coyote couple had visited a winter-killed moose — twisted and frozen as though it had died crumpled up. The moose also served as a rendezvous point, a protein windfall. Lines of solitary tracks radiated out from the carcass. For the rest of the winter (which extends well into April north of the Presidential Range), the eastern coyotes chiseled away at moose meat.

Last winter, as Linny and I drove south on Interstate 91, five miles below the Wells River exit a large DOR blocked the passing lane. It was well past 11:00 P.M. and the night was moonless and overcast. I backed up, with the bright beams shining for a closer look. But before I reached the carcass, something sidetracked me. Halfway down the sandy slope next to the passing lane my headlights caught yellow eye-shine in a patch of scrubby vegetation. A coyote, no doubt taking advantage of the DOR. As I stopped the car, the unassuming animal left the hillside, walked toward the DOR, then sat down to assess my intentions. I eased the car forward. The coyote sprung to its feet, and to my surprise, so did the DOR. What we thought was a road-killed deer was in fact a male coyote, curled and asleep on the interstate. Both animals moved off the road and up the hill, their yellow eyes flashing in the headlights.

The knoll between Interstates 91's north- and southbound lanes stretched for almost a mile. Its loose, well-drained sandy soil — a vestige of the Ice Age, where glacial melt-water had deposited sediments — made an ideal den site for the coyotes. They could easily dig their own or fashion one started by a red fox or woodchuck. Across the southbound lane the land tapered toward a small marshy drainage, and above the northbound lane a forest of pointed spruce and fir climbed the hills, scratching the horizon for miles. This was unqualified eastern coyote country. It was not as wild as the Upper Ammonoosuc, but with its broken land, friable soil — easily dug and facing the afternoon sun — and shield provided by the traffic, the animals were safe from guns and traps on their island habitat.

Come spring, the interstate would provide a sumptuous buffet laid out with raccoons and woodchucks, skunks and squirrels, pancake mice, muskrats, maybe even a deer or two.

One morning several years ago I watched a male coyote lope along the floodplain of the Connecticut River, a robust animal moving against a terraced hillside. He took woodchucks and voles in the fertile bottomland and chased hare through the alder swamps where spring flood waters collected in potholes, dwelling less than two hundred yards from the center of Haverhill. When the coyote spotted me he ran with long, bounding strides across the verdant fields, his tail parallel to the ground. Flocks of robins flushed and scattered killdeer screamed. Somewhere above the high-water line on the wooded hill the coyote's mate nursed four to seven gray, woolly pups. He was the provider, she the defender, the mother whose warm, wet tongue cleaned and soothed, whose muffled voice, sagging nipples, and deep canine smell were the pups' bridge to life beyond their closed eyes.

Fifteen miles south of Haverhill, a couple of hundred yards from the Lyme green, behind a white church in the sand bank where the road crew gathers gravel to keep the town's roads passable in winter, another family of eastern coyotes made their home. I've never seen them; they're much too cautious, living as they do in the heart of town. After a spring snow, however, the sand pit — another by-product of glacial melt-water — is scrawled with coyote calligraphy, and on cold March nights I've heard their serenade. The coyotes howl back to dogs, fire, police, and ambulance sirens, and to the long mid-night whistle of the train as it passes across the river. They send their voices through the crooked pines and past the weathered headstones that flank the north end of the sand pit. Together the coyotes, the train, and the dogs produce a wild symphony. But without the coyotes' high-pitched wail and falsetto yips the music would fall short of its brilliance.

I'm not surprised that eastern coyotes eavesdrop on Lyme and Haverhill, for these adaptable wanderers walk with light steps, and except for occasional bursts of exuberance they conceal their presence. It is a good thing, for as a culture we have never come to terms with

other predators, particularly large ones, and in an act self-deprecation
we have done our best to rid North America of its wolves and lions.
Vermont lost her last wolf in 1902, New Hampshire in 1895. Mountain lions, quieter, hung on longer in the Granite State. On
Thanksgiving Day in 1881, a 182 1/2-pound lion — called a "cata-
mount" in the Northeast — was shot in Barnard. It was the largest
of the fewer than twenty lions ever taken in Vermont. It was also
the last taken. During the 1920s two lions roamed northern New
Hampshire along the east bank of the Androscoggin River from Cambridge to Lake Umbagog. A third left its tracks in the soft loam of
the Green Mountains in 1934. Both the wolf and the lion crave
venison, and neither has thinned the deer herd, here or anywhere
else. In fact, most wildlife biologists agree that the number and
availability of prey determines the survival rate of predators, and
thereby controls them. Not the other way around.

It wasn't long ago that the howl of wolves and the screeching of
catamounts rode the night currents. The hills and the river remember,
and the deer, without predators to weed the chaff from the herd,
have had their fitness compromised. Eastern coyotes eat some deer,
but they are not big-game predators. Fawns and adults indisposed
by disease, injury, starvation, or deep snow, are sometimes taken.
More often the venison in a coyote's diet, George Wiggins not-
withstanding, has been scavenged from deer wasted by dogs or from
road kills or gunshot animals.

After the first deep snow, white-tailed deer, which have been strung
across their summer range, convene for winter on a hill with a
southern exposure and plenty of hemlock for browsing and holding
back the snow. Deeryards invite attention. Eastern coyotes, bobcats,
fishers, and sometimes bears clean up winter kills, and if the snow
is so deep that it impedes the progress of deer, a coyote or bobcat
may make a relatively easy kill. Dogs visit deeryards, too. If tracking is poor and the carcass chewed up, it is difficult to tell whether
a deer died of starvation or whether it was starving when it was
brought down by a predator or a dog. In an effort to appease hunters
who claimed coyotes were annihilating game, the Maine Fish and
Wildlife Department set out snares in several crowded yards. The

snares worked, but instead of coyotes, the wardens caught dogs
and deer.

Vermont Fish and Wildlife Department biologists used their annual deer-mortality records between 1969 and 1985 to indict both
dogs and cars as the two leading causes of the state's nonhunting
deer deaths. Domestic dogs destroyed 8,227 deer, while cars clipped
another 28,565. Coyotes and bobcats killed and consumed 1,234 deer,
less than 3 percent of the combined figure for dogs and cars. If we
persecuted our cars and dogs with the same vehemence with which
we hammer coyotes, speed limits would plunge, and dogs would be
forever leashed.

A stocky beagle sat in the back seat wagging his tail as Bob Rooks,
the local game warden, drove toward the Hartford Landfill. A young
man dedicated to his profession, Rooks had become a warden because
he loved to hunt and fish, but worked such long days that he had
little time for his avocations. I couldn't imagine how the beagle could
pull down a deer, but he had done so three times. Twice his master
had been warned about his dog's odious behavior, and at the moment that was all that mattered. The dump master knew the warden
and the warden's business, for Bob had brought deer killers to the
dump all winter. I stared into the beagle's big, wet eyes, so dark and
soulful they belied the truth. Bob held the dog at arm's length with
a rigid metal leash, withdrew his revolver, and shot once at point-
blank range. The beagle fell, his blood spilling on garbage. It was
the eighth dog Rooks had killed that winter, and it wasn't to be
the last.

The winter of 1982 was tough on northern New England deer.
Vermont alone estimated that fifteen thousand had been dragged
down by dogs or run ragged until they dropped, and this figure,
said the warden, was conservative. I spent the rest the afternoon with
Bob Rooks as he answered call after call about dogs chasing deer.
We snowshoed into a Taftsville yard where a collie had chased deer
down a steep slope, through pine, and across a meadow thigh-high
with snow. For the deer, conditions were terrible. Their pointed
hooves broke through the crust and sank several feet into the snow;

the collie, her weight more evenly spread, padded over the surface. I followed the collie's tracks as she singled out a deer, driving it across the meadow, over the highway, and onto the frozen Ottauquechee River, where, after a quarter-mile run, the dog got bored and went home. No deer died then, but death is often bloodless.

By late March deer are thin, their preferred browse — hemlock, sumac, and red maple — is in short supply, and the energy necessary to escape a dog taxes their already meager fat reserves. The Taftsville yard was overbrowsed. Hemlocks were stripped of their lower branches, while melting snow dropped the deer below the remaining soft, green needles. Faced with empty bellies, the deer browsed white pine, a useless food that appeases a nagging hunger without yielding a lick of nutrition. Does who are carrying unborn twin fawns suffer a double hardship: with high nutritional needs, they must conserve their energy and pace themselves through the critical days of waning snow. Four of the five carcasses we autopsied were does; three held seeds of the next generation. Late in the day we visited a yard in the Tiger Town section of West Hartford, a remote corner of the Upper Valley. After trekking a mile along a spiraling snowmobile trail, we found another deer carcass. A dog on the throat, another on the rump, she had been dragged down, disemboweled, and left to decay on red snow.

In 1983, 1,791 garden-browsing deer were killed by Vermont landowners, more than the total known lost to wildlife predators over the past eighteen years. Also that year, at least another 379 deer were shot out of season. Every winter I find evidence of a deer or two shot and butchered out of season. Yet still the tale is promulgated that coyotes are to blame for the decrease in Vermont and New Hampshire deer. A neighbor tells me that in the 1960s, before coyotes were common, he saw 30 or 40 deer each evening in the hills above the White River. I don't doubt there were more deer in the 1960s. There were much fewer people and dogs, too. Second homes were novel, condominiums unheard of, fewer people owned snowmobiles, and still fewer raced their machines through the woods, driving deer from the yards. A state biologist told me that the intersection of

Interstates 91 and 89 in White River Junction severed Vermont's best deer habitat.

If a finger is to be pointed at the cause for the decline of white-tailed deer, we ought to point it at ourselves and let the coyote be. One dark February night during my first winter in the Upper Valley, Linny's big, friendly dog, Maury, came home with the thigh of a deer. Two days later a couple of hooves littered the driveway, and a week after that we shipped Maury back to Linny's brother in suburban Kentucky. All of us are at fault, and as long as our wildlands are pillaged and plundered by development (and by dogs) and as long as people fixate on their predator biases, there will be fewer and fewer deer. Fewer coyotes, too.

Shepherds hate coyotes with the same passion that hunters do. Every year New Hampshire and Vermont reimburse farmers for livestock depredations. Coyotes cause some of the damage, black bears some, but again dogs are the real culprit. In the 1870s dogs ravaged sheep to such an extent that Vermont farmers, teetering on the edge of bankruptcy, butchered their flocks to prevent further losses. There were no coyotes to blame then. Of course, the coyote does not lie down with the lamb. Not quite. They are opportunistic predators, and when confronted by a flock of fat, stupid prey, there can be trouble. When a coyote makes a kill it faces the ewe or lamb, grabs it by the throat and severs its windpipe, suffocating it. Feeding begins at the flanks, and the coyotes return night after night until only wool and bone are left. Dogs, on the other hand, rip sheeps' hind quarters, spilling both bowels and blood, and if they feed — which is indeed rare — they begin with the anus. There are ways of protecting sheep from coyote attack: electric fences work, and so do sheep dogs, particularly a Yugoslavian breed popular in the West and in Massachusetts. Since eastern coyotes are crepuscular, sheep should be brought in at night, or at least pastured close to the house. Sheep bells help, too.

Only a small percentage of coyotes are sheep killers. Indiscriminate hunting, trapping, and poisoning affect not only the outlaws but also the inoffensive coyotes, as well as foxes, bobcats, and fishers. Besides, coyotes are smart and not easily controlled. In 1969 Arizona declared war on all coyotes, spending an estimated $157,603 to avenge $42,211 worth of damage. Coyotes still howl from the rim rock. Ranchers from the Canadian prairie provinces employ what many wildlife biologists believe is the most effective method to dissuade nuisance coyotes, lithium chloride. Mutton and beef sprinkled with lithium is scattered on the edge of a meadow. When coyotes eat the bait they get sick and wretch, their memories burn, and the knowledge spreads from generation to generation until the desire for lamb chops and veal is lost.

From Pitcher Mountain's fire tower in south-central New Hampshire one can see Mount Ascutney and the Connecticut River valley to the west and Mount Monadnock to the southeast. In every direction there is water — lakes, rivers, and ponds peeking from behind a maze of hills. On a clear day, after a cold front has swept across New Hampshire, Mount Washington emerges from its crown of clouds and stands against the northwest horizon.

For most of the 1970s, Harry Hammond kept the fire watch on Pitcher Mountain. He is stout and friendly, a real chatterbox. If Harry wasn't talking with the hikers who had climbed for the view or to pick blueberries or to watch migrating hawks, or if he wasn't scanning for smoke, he read Louis L'Amour novels, counted hawks himself, and kept track of a coyote family that patrolled the mountain and rich pasture to the south. I became acquainted with Harry in the fall of 1975. We talked at length about life in a state without an income tax, about the black bears that came to the mountain each August to fatten on blueberries, and about coyotes. Harry knew something about eastern coyotes, and I — after a year and a half of studying them in southwest Texas, collecting and analyzing their scat in an aborted attempt at a Ph.D. — knew something about western coyotes. As we compared notes, we discovered that in terms of coyote behavior, east was east and west was west.

In the West, coyotes are noisy. Their plaintive voices are the song of the desert, the prairie, and the high plateau. All night, every night they carried on, and I would lay awake, curled in my sleeping bag, listening to the chorus. In early spring the male and female formed a duet, broadcasting their nuptials across the sandstone desert. In summer, half-grown pups joined the chorus, and a family of five or six coyotes harmonized with a lone howl, usually that of the male on a hunting foray calling from some crumbling mesa. At times, when several families at once raised their voices from separate choir lofts, the desert night rocked. Harry said eastern coyotes sing, but are much less vocal and unpredictable, except in late winter while pair bonds form, and rarely, he added, do more than two lift their voices together. Sandra Miller, my mammal-feeding friend from Hanover, agrees. Like Harry Hammond, she is a devotee of the eastern coyote, and she once kept track of a family that spent the winter under the floor boards of an old house site. Except to eat and pant, she tells me, the coyotes kept their mouths shut.

The best part of visiting Harry was watching the coyotes in the dawn fog, mousing among Scotch Highland cattle. While the cattle grazed, the coyotes pounced. Foxlike, they leapt into the air, jack-knifed in midflight, and landed forefeet first, attempting to pin a vole to the ground. If the pounce was successful, the vole was flung into the air, caught, bit, and swallowed; if unsuccessful, the coyote leaned toward the grass, listening and waiting for another chance, or moved ten or fifteen yards away to start again.

That winter the fire tower was closed, so Harry sat at home in Keene reading more Louis L'Amour novels, while I snowshoed after the Pitcher Mountain coyotes. In deep snow, they left the pasture for the woods, often hunting in pairs. One afternoon I found where a snowshoe hare had been flushed from under a sweep of low hemlock. One coyote kept up the chase, the other hid behind a sugar maple. As the hare grew tired, the second coyote replaced the first, and in short order the hare fell. Teamwork, I reported to Harry.

In west Texas coyotes hunted in pairs, too, chasing jackrabbits across the flats, ambushing woodrats and kangaroo rats from behind mesquite and creosote bushes. From their scat, I found they ate gophers and ground squirrels, several species of mice, snakes and lizards, fruit and insects — grasshoppers, beetles, and crickets — and once in a while, a scorpion. Whether western or eastern, coyotes are opportunistic, catholic feeders. In the East, besides hare and meadow voles, carrion and the occasional deer or sheep, coyotes enjoy woodchucks, cottontails, white-footed and deer mice, jumping mice (both woodland and meadow), bog lemmings (both northern and southern), rock voles, red-backed voles, pine voles, porcupines, muskrats, beaver, chipmunks, all kinds of squirrels (gray and red, northern and southern flying), skunks, mink, both species of weasel, ruffed and spruce grouse, turkey, mallards, black and wood ducks, any songbirds that nest or feed close to the ground, snapping turtles and their eggs, snakes (garter, milk, water, and black), bullfrogs, green frogs, wood frogs, leopard frogs, any species of fish they can get a hold of, crayfish, crickets, grasshoppers, land snails, centipedes, acorns, pine nuts, beechnuts, apples, berries (blue, straw, black, and rasp), chokecherries, grass, cheese, French fries, tinfoil, wax paper and gauze. In Texas they have such a fondness for watermelons that many farmers claim coyotes can tell when a melon is ripe. In the East they have a taste for green corn and cantaloupe. Among the many interesting items about coyote natural history found in a fact sheet published by the Vermont Fish and Wildlife Department, there is a note about a Sudbury farmer who shot a crazed young coyote in his pasture. The coyote had been racing around, zig-zagging and jumping like Walter Peyton, and snapping his jaws as though in distress. A department biologist autopsied the animal and found its stomach crammed with red-legged grasshoppers.

Less than a century has slipped by since the river and the hills and the deer knew wolves. They're all listening again, the river, the hills, the deer, and me, to the wild, wondrous serenades of the coyote. I cannot help but respect coyotes for their tenacity in the face of blind hatred, for their ability to live anywhere and to eat anything, and for their resourcefulness. Like the Pilgrims they came to New England, survived, and flourished.

9

FOX WATCHING OFF ROUTE 5

THAT DARK FEBRUARY NIGHT, one of those rare midwinter nights when the sky is clear and the temperature above freezing, I heard a fox call — a short run of sharp yips and barks, then a long, emaciated howl, smaller and daintier than the wild, drawn out voice of a coyote. From the darkness beyond our peeper marsh, near the meadow's head where the land rises gently toward the ridge, another volley of barks and yips rose above the tree tops and carried onto our porch.

All winter this fox had marked the snow, but tonight, as Orion climbed in the southern sky, he uncurled and stretched and sent an urgent message into the night. He never used a winter den. He slept in the middle of the meadow instead, head to the wind so the long outer fur of the guard hairs — rust-colored and silky — stayed still. Beneath those long protective hairs a wrap of dense under-wool held a warm envelope of air. Once his blood began to flow and his leg muscles loosened, the fox wandered into the night. After several steps he squirted urine on a withered milkweed stem then headed for a small pond tucked into a fold in the meadow. With his urine the fox had run a classified advertisement, announcing both his presence and his desire. More drops down the side of a cattail stalk.

Fox piss is strong stuff that has a faint skunky smell, and he used it like semiprecious fluid — a few drops here, a few drops there — the pungent odor clinging to snow, stems, and cold air until it is washed away. If it is fresh, I can smell fox piss without bending down. But if it's old, then my dog — who can read weathered urine — knows that a cunning (and horny) predator slightly bigger than a tabby has passed through the meadow. Five weeks before the equinox, as an annual jolt of testosterone coursed through the fox's body, he sought company, attempting to reestablish a pair bond with last year's vixen or to attract a new mate by pissing everywhere. His trail stained the snow and the air.

After marking the cattail the fox strode off along the edge of the pond, twice backtracking, when he heard tiny footfalls beneath the snow. At the head of a track pattern that resembled a buckled figure eight the fox crouched. He pinpointed a mouse by leaning into the sound, an ear cocked toward the ground, then drove up off his long thin hind legs straight into the air. At the height of the jump he jackknifed and his front paws struck the ground first, pinning a mouse securely beneath them.

According to J. David Henry, a wildlife biologist from northern Saskatchewan who has unraveled a great many vulpine mysteries, red fox are built for these quiet airborne attacks . Using simple physics to prove his point, Henry compared the skeletons of a male fox and a male coyote. According to the principle of *surface area to volume ratio*, if a wooden block doubles its linear dimensions the volume and weight increase by eight. Applied to mammals, a proportional increase in surface area per gram of limb bone should exist between fox and coyote, which also pounce. Henry found, however, that red foxes had 30 percent more surface area than the rule of squares and cubes predicts. Which is to say that red foxes have longer, lighter legs than one would expect for an animal of their size. They are, so to speak, the gymnasts of the canines, airborne little dogs that can float past the antipredator defenses of small mammals. They are lighter and comparatively leaner than coyotes.

The fox's four thin, daggerlike canine teeth punctured the mouse. In a gulp it was gone. From spring to pounce to bite, the fox had dispatched his prey with catlike precision. Red foxes, although members of the dog family, have several anatomical traits that converge with those of cats: their claws are semiretractable; their pupils are vertically slit and the *tapetum lucidum*, that iridescent eye membrane that recycles light before it leaves the eyes and is the source of an animal's eye-shine, is well developed; their canine teeth, long and thin, are proportionally not as thick as those of coyotes. With all of these catlike qualities and with its comparative lightness, it is no wonder the fox launched into the air when it went after the mouse. Only when hunting snowshoe hare, woodchucks, or other moderately sized prey did he chase them doglike.

Hare were scarce this winter, so Reynard padded through the snow, listening. His single line of tracks etched across the pond and meadow and up the apron of the ridge. A wider-chested animal, a raccoon for instance, would have marked the snow with all four feet while a long, thin, short-legged animal, a fisher or a weasel, would leave a series of parallel prints. But when the long-legged, thin-chested fox walked, his hind feet swung directly into the tracks of his forefeet. When he ran, all four feet marked the snow. I once shadowed a fox along the curve of a frozen brook. When it realized I was coming, it broke into a dead run. Its tracks, at first a leisurely line of prints spaced eight to twelve inches apart, exploded into clusters of four, deeper and more pronounced, with seven- to eight-foot gaps between them. But I was hours behind this fox, so he moved with assurance, varying his speed to suit his mood.

Wind had cleared the crest of snow, exposing frozen ground unattractive to voles and unpromising for the fox. He crossed the ridge and headed down the south slope through beech-maple woods, pausing only to piss. In the woods the snow was deeper and travel slower, so the fox plowed instead of padded, his long fluffy tail dusting the surface. Halfway down the ridge he caught scent of a vixen that had crossed the head of an adjoining meadow. His pace hastened. With ears bent forward, he yapped — short, sharp yaps — then pranced like a frisky colt. Alongside a prostrate sugar maple, amid a highway of deer mouse prints, the vixen had left her mark, a few drops of bright red estrus blood amid a splash of golden-yellow urine. Color coordination had no effect upon the fox. Like sensitive black-and-white film, his eyes registered only shades of gray. He knew from the blood's rich odor that the vixen, too, was ready to breed. Casting prudence aside, he howled and screeched then followed her footsteps.

By early morning he had crossed a brook along the back corner of an idle dairy farm, nearly a mile and a half from the ridge. A single set of tracks marked the snow. Her scent grew fresher, almost overpowering. Again the fox barked and yipped, waggling his tail in anticipation. A long line of prints snaked through the pasture. At the end sat the vixen. A dome of arctic air settled over east-central Vermont, warding off snow. The wind picked up, temperatures plunged. Dry snow swirled off the meadow into tiny frozen twisters that skirted the surface then vanished. And beneath that vaulted February sky, now flush with the rising sun, two red foxes came together.

Late one day in May, just past 9:00 P.M., I saw the fox pups. With binoculars I followed their silhouettes as they pranced and bounced along the crest of the hill. When the pups stopped moving they faded into the hill like shadows. No movement, no foxes. The vixen was around but I never saw her. She glided through the woods on the far side of the hill, a specter of the night. A twig snapped. A shadow barked. I measured her presence and influence by the movement of the kits. Every rustle drew their attention, and when she spoke they froze. The vixen ran a tight but odd ship.

Her den's main entrance was sixty feet from Route 5 — a popular state highway that parallels the Connecticut River — and fifteen feet from the Boston-Maine railroad tracks. The ground trembles for half a mile, and the Lyme coyotes across the river sing whenever the midnight train whistles through. At fifteen feet away, tucked in a blind passage four feet below the ground, I imagined what the rumble of the train might register on the Richter scale. A hundred yards north of the den the hillside flattens into a broad alfalfa field, and to the south a tangled slope of brambles and perennials runs for more

than a mile. Beyond the main entrance to the den, on the eastern side of the hill and behind the brambles a small corridor of woods extends to the Connecticut River. Across Route 5 there are farms and ponds, a meadow and a belt of white pine. Her territory was varied, the game abundant. Besides the train and the highway there is the clanking of farm equipment from the hay fields down by the river. Bicycles and canoes pass by all day long. Yet the vixen and her family — three pups and the dog — subsisted in the center of this hectic rural world.

Red fox live throughout most of North America, from the high arctic into the southeastern lowlands, by-passing only the arid Southwest and coastal California. When I studied mammals at Ball State University, we called the North American red fox *Vulpes fulva*, which distinguished it as a separate species from the Eurasian red fox, *Vulpes vulpes*. Both sprang from a common ancestor sometime during the Pleistocene epoch. Now the relationship between the two species of red fox is clouded. Most authorities agree that red foxes — like short-tailed and least weasels, timber wolves, wolverines, moose, caribou, and brown (grizzly) bears — are the same species on both sides of the Pacific. Since the Old World fox was described first, the name *Vulpes vulpes* has replaced *Vulpes fulva*. What complicates the issue, however, is that some biologists suggest that prior to the arrival of Europeans, the red fox was absent or scarce over much of North America. In the middle of the eighteenth century European colonists, missing the sport of kings, brought the Eurasian red fox to America, and over the next fifty years the animals spread throughout southern New England and the Middle Atlantic States. If foxes were present prior to these introductions, then the animals here now are mongrels — hybrids with both Old and New World blood.

Which version is not quite clear. Audubon and Bachman believed that in the mideighteenth century a large part of America was without red foxes. A century later, they had reached as far south as Georgia. Supporting Audubon and Bachman's claim are pre-Columbian fossils taken from Pennsylvania caves and Indian digs that are all assigned to gray, not red, foxes. So where was the North American red fox at the time the Mayflower dropped anchor? They were to the north, beyond latitude forty or forty-five, says Charles Churcher, the acknowledged expert on the subject. Bone fragments from woodland Indian sites in Ontario are assigned to the wolf, coyote, and gray fox, and a very few to the red fox. But, says Churcher, more red fox remains are dated earlier — from the tenth to the fourteenth centuries — than from the fifteenth to the seventeeth centuries which may mean a warming trend sent them farther north into the evergreen hinterlands of Canada, as deciduous forests and their attendant gray foxes marched northward.

Since latitude forty-five cuts across northern Vermont, my foxes may have had native blood in their veins. But I doubt it. Living as they did between a rock and hard place, they must have been like me, descended from "flatlanders." When I returned the next afternoon, all three pups were lying in the sun on a bare patch of ground just below the crest of the hill. They paid no attention to my car until the door swung open. Then they plunged downhill, disappearing into their burrow as though sucked into the ground.

The main entrance to the burrow was hidden from the road by a saddle of packed soil. I assembled my camera gear and waited. In a few minutes a pair of ears poked up from the saddle. Then a nose. More ears. And eventually, three pups. They were gray and dull rusty-brown, the color of bare earth, and blended into the hillside so well that bicyclists slowing down to inspect my activity never noticed them. Once the pups emerged from behind the saddle, they shed their fears and began to play. One batted around a piece of woodchuck hide, while the other two gently chewed and pawed at each other's face. As long as I kept my distance they paid no attention to me. To them my laughter was no more threatening than the wind or the whine of tires along Route 5. At times I found it hard to stop laughing. The pups had no sense of balance and only a rudimentary sense of the principles of gravity. As their play became more frenzied, one pup leaped onto the other and they tumbled off the saddle, head-over-heels downhill. The solitary pup, too, had a hard time staying on all fours. Twice he took a break from the woodchuck hide and started scratching so vigorously that he fell over and rolled downhill as well.

Red fox pups, born blind and helpless, are covered with a dense grayish-brown wool, and except for their white-tipped tails there is little to recommend them as red foxes. Although their eyes open in nine days and they walk in three weeks, they stay below ground for their first month. Great horned owls pose the biggest threat to unwary or unguarded fox pups, although dogs, coyotes, and fishers may snatch a few. A friend, a New Hampshire bear guide, once found a bobcat with a red fox pup in its mouth. It was fair play, he said, for the year before he spotted a fox trotting across a meadow with a bobcat kitten clamped in its jaws. Adult foxes may move their family two or three times before the pups are six weeks old. Often a litter is split between two dens, which reduces the concentration of external parasites like fleas and ticks and ensures that a catastrophe will not wipe out the entire litter at once. When the pups are moved their play things — wings and bones and hides — go with them.

I guessed the pups to be seven weeks old. Their den, as I far as I could tell, was their birthplace. Red foxes may use a den over and over, sometimes for generations. Once when I was hiking along an esker on the west side of Hudson Bay I found a fox den system littered with Canada goose feathers and bones. Of the seven burrows that cut into the shallow esker, five appeared active and each of these, I imagine, radiated from a central nursery like the arms of an octopus. A companion from a nearby village told me that the den had been in use for fifteen years. A fox Linny and I had raised, on the other hand, dug three dens in a single summer, with no articulating tunnels between them, and used each den according to a foxy schedule that made no sense to me.

When a plane passed over, the three pups stopped playing and watched with rapt attention. Cars and trucks had no effect on them (not yet, anyway). Neither did bicycles. But a bark or a yip from a parent triggered a mad rush to the burrow or sent them scrambling over the crest of the hill, into the woods, and down a rear entrance to their den. Fox dens have several entrances. Often the pups would enter the saddle and reappear on the top of the hill. Late that fall, months after the family had dispersed, I crossed the tracks and found their rear entrance. An auxiliary burrow fashioned beneath the grafted roots of an old paper birch led back thirty feet into the hill. This was no record for fox excavation; they are known to dig tunnel systems that are over seventy-five feet long. In 1981 Linny and I received an orphaned male red fox pup from a neighbor. Socks (we named the pup in honor of Dr. Suess) dug a labyrinthine tunnel system in his pen. Whenever I entered, I measured my steps, for no matter where I stood I sank through the thin roof of a fox tunnel.

Although I kept my distance from the wild foxes' home, I could tell by the deep trails that cut through the grasses and brambles that this was not the first generation of pups to watch the cars pass along Route 5 or to be rocked awake by the thunder of trains. For years foxes have been drawn to this sandy hillside. There is a diversity of cover and plenty of food. The earth is easy to dig, and the railroad tracks make an easy path to the far reaches of the foxes' territory. If the fox pups could handle the noise and avoid being hit by a car, they'd have it made. I was wrong.

Later that afternoon I spotted the vixen on the railroad tracks. She had been hunting in the pasture north of the burrow and was heading home with a mole in her mouth. Her gait was strange, for with each step she hitched to the right as though walking half on, half off some imaginary curb. When whe came just below the burrow, the vixen started up the hill. She limped. As she drew parallel to my car, I saw that she moved with more than a limp, a three-legged hobble. Her right foot was missing, chewed off, probably, in desperation to escape from a leg-hold trap. I have seen it happen before, both with foxes and coyotes. I once put down a tortured west Texas coyote that had shred all the skin and muscle from a hind leg in an attempt to rid himself of a trap. Compared to that coyote, the vixen was lucky. Local trappers insisted that the vixen's leg got shot off during deer season, or that maybe she had stepped on glass or gotten run over by a train. No matter how the loss occurred, the fox's pouncing days were behind her.

The red fox is more adaptable than the gray fox. Grays are woodland animals, natives of the New World that live throughout most of the lower forty-eight states, except in the northern Rocky Mountains and on the treeless Great Plains. They tolerate hot, dry conditions better than red foxes do and range much farther south, through Mexico and Central America. But where the two foxes meet, the red has the upper hand. When the eastern hardwood forests were cleared, the red fox followed the pioneer farmers west, and to a certain extent displaced the native gray fox. Both foxes prefer a diversity of habitat but the gray fox, a tree climber, needs big woods with leaning trees. So when the timber fell, the gray suffered.

Red foxes have made a transition to suburban living — although to a lesser extent than raccoons and opossums — something a gray fox would find oppressive. (I've watched two families of grays, however, at two different locations on the New Hampshire side of the Connecticut River, regularly accept handouts of white bread and doughnuts at backyard bird feeders, delighting the respective home owners.) There are red fox in Nassau County, Long Island. I still find their signs by the ocean, trails through the sand dunes, scat tightly packed with the pits and skin of beach plums, the bones and fur of cottontails and meadow voles, the feathers of nestling gulls and terns, even the scales of beached fish. When the shore is crammed with sun-bathers, the foxes sleep in the dunes. When the sun sets and people leave, they stir. Few suspect they're there. Although they no longer live in the midst of tract housing, red fox still roam the large state parks — Bethpage, Muttontown, and Caumsett. On the north shore of Nassau County red fox do well. The large estates with their woods and fields and salt marshes are just what the fox likes. Everything is private and protected.

I've watched red fox on the eastern end of Long Island where the truck farms meet the sea. One night along a farm road in Orient Point, not far from the state park, a fox loped ahead of my car. It had not the slightest concern for the vehicle and kept up its pace for several hundred yards before veering off the road. Early in the morning the red fox of Montauk Point go down to the pond just west of the lighthouse, where I've seen them slipping through the bayberry and poison ivy tangles, more apparitions than mammals. In New York City red fox take shelter in the big woods that border the Bronx River and are sometimes spotted crossing Fordham Road between the New York Botanical Garden and the Bronx Zoo. A few may still live on Staten Island. But the gray fox is long gone from the city, and on Long Island he is rare indeed, if he exists at all.

I returned to the railroad tracks and found some bleached woodchuck bones and damaged mallard feathers the following spring, but no sign of the foxes. The hillside lay idle. Ranks of horsetails and sensitive ferns crowded the saddle, and the mouth of the burrow, widened by snow-melt and rain, was plugged with leaves and crossed with cobwebs. Even the many local skunks dug elsewhere, fashioning their own dens rather than renovating the foxes' abandoned site. After hearing of my interest in red foxes, two kids at a Montshire Museum program reported that a pair with pups lived on their parents' dairy farm half a mile south of the empty den I had recently checked. The foxes were active all day, they said, and were easy to watch. They had already approached celebrity status among the kids of Norwich. A Brownie troop, the farmer's five children, and all of their friends enjoyed fox watching. So did the farmer.

J. David Henry, in his brilliant little book, *Red Fox: The Catlike Canine*, attributes the den selection to the vixen, who visits several potential sites on the territory, cleaning out each before choosing a whelping den. After surveying thirty-five whelping dens, Henry found several intrinsic characteristics: red foxes prefer sandy soil, often in the woods but close to a meadow and water, usually within one hundred yards of a lake, river, or as Henry calls it, a "humble pool." Dens may be used repeatedly, following a matriarchal line of descent (as that Hudson Bay den evidently was), or abandoned then renovated after one or more years of vacancy.

The three-legged vixen was not at the new den. Dead, I assumed. One of the vixen's daughters and the father, or perhaps a brother or wayfaring young male looking for a territory, had claimed the neighborhood and had made the decision to forsake the railroad den site for the sloped pasture of the dairy farm. Again, there were three pups. And again, I kept abreast of their domestic affairs; there were three dens this year. The first den, the largest and most prominent of their three homes, occupied a choice piece of property. The main entrance, a third of the way up the knoll, faced the Connecticut River so that when the sun moved above the New Hampshire hills it warmed the brown earth and the brown pups. Above the ground a worn footpath threaded the front door to the back. Below, a tunnel with barely enough elbow room for an adult red fox led into the den and out the back door.

In front of the main entrance to the first den, a large mound of earth — a piazza of sorts — looked out upon a cow pasture, a farm road, and a small tangle of trees. The vixen, who often rested in a gully at the base of the knoll, knew every footstep of every cow and every shuffle of the farm children. And the dog fox, yellowish-red like fresh-plowed earth, sat at the crest of the knoll where he could see the farm door slam or the tractor start. There was no surprising the fox family.

Their home was a stolen one. The original architect and builder was a woodchuck, now deceased. The red foxes ate the woodchuck (as red fox often do) and left its shredded hide for the pups to cut their teeth on. During the second week in May the foxes moved off the grassy knoll and renovated yet another den. Their second home, across the farm road and midway up a wooded slope, faced the pasture. Here the foxes were in deep shade until 11:00 A.M., when less than two hours of filtered sunlight began to sprinkle through the canopy. This lair had two entrances twenty feet apart, both only fifty feet from the farm road and easy to watch. The entrances were guarded by the exposed roots of a balsam fir and a big white pine, as though the foxes meant to hold back larger animals — coyotes, perhaps, or the farm dogs.

The new home was perfect. There were no heavy-footed cows, no noisy grackles and red-winged blackbirds, and as the days grew hotter and stickier, the pups stayed cool in the shade. At first I found them close to their burrows, yawning, stretching, and pouncing like kittens. Later, when they began to explore the wooded hillside, I heard their footsteps shuffling through the fallen leaves. If something startled the pups, they rushed toward the fir — half running, half sliding — and dove between the roots. In a moment, a pair of little ears and a moist black nose poked back out, as though the pups were playing peekaboo.

Early one morning as I sat in my car watching the pups play, three crows broke the silence with a loud volley of caws. The woods and pasture rang with their discordant calls. I could see them now and again through a weft of branches, black and noisy above the hill. They announced that a predator had marched into the open across the upper pasture. I never heard the fox bark or detected any sudden breaks in the pattern of dappled sunlight, but I know the language of crows, and this agitated cawing was a predator alarm. The pups knew this too as they ran up the wooded slope to meet their parent.

The first pup up got the prize, a half-grown ruffed grouse. He seized the limp bird in his mouth and trotted toward the den, half-blinded by the grouse's wings which bounced back and forth across his eyes like a Mardi gras mask. The other two pups were right behind, scrambling after their breakfast. Out of the corner of my eye I saw the male walking up the farm road. Within twenty feet of my car, he stopped and stared. In his mouth was a vole. The crows had missed this fox; the pups hadn't. Inside the den, feasting on grouse, they had sensed through some form of clairvoyance that their father was nearby. All three pups left the den at once and reassembled by the spruce. The male padded into the woods, climbed the hill, then as silent and deliberate as a scout covering his trail, he turned about and walked back down to his family. One meadow vole does not go a long way with three red fox pups. But this spring the meadow vole population had peaked. They were everywhere and easy to catch. I caught three by hand, one in the front yard as I mowed the lawn. And almost nightly on the interstate, plump little voles — the rolly-pollies of the rodent world — scooted in front of my car. Linny even ran one over.

As far as I could tell voles accounted for most of the red foxes' diet. Each thin, tapering scat I examined consisted of vole fur and vole bones, and sometimes teeth. Vole molars, with their distinctive sigmoid cusps, were easy to recognize. Uncut meadows, tall and green with hints of golden Alexander, harbored hundreds of voles an acre. To the dairy farmer, vole-eating foxes were welcome neighbors, for meadow voles — the most prolific mammal in North America and perhaps the world — eat lots of grass.

Meadow voles have a hard-to-define breeding season. Any month suits them. Eight to ten litters a year with one to ten young per litter is the norm, but a captive vole once produced seventeen litters in a year, for a total of eighty-three young. One of her offspring followed up with thirteen litters totaling seventy-eight young before she was a year old. Gestation is about twenty-one days, and female young are fertile in three weeks, males in eight. Meadow voles have such an amazing reproductive potential that were it not for predators, fires, flood, and disease they would overrun the earth. Everything eats meadow voles — red and gray foxes, coyotes, bobcats, black bears, fishers, long- and short-tailed weasels, mink, skunk, otter, raccoons, opossums, dogs, cats, short-tailed shrews, all of the hawks and owls, three species of gulls, crows, ravens, blue jays, northern shrikes, great blue and green-backed herons, American bitterns, milk snakes, water snakes, garter snakes, black racers, timber rattlesnakes, bullfrogs, green frogs, and, when voles enter the water, even fish — bass, pickerel, pike, and big trout.

According to a friend who enjoys numbers as much as voles, a single pair of meadow voles and their descendants — barring mortality of any kind — producing an average of 5 young per litter could increase by 38,912 at the end one year and 236,000,000 at the end of two. Within three years there would be enough meadow voles to completely cover the state of New Hampshire from the bottom of Lake Winnipesaukee to the top of Mount Washington. And if their exponential growth continued unchecked, voles could carpet the land masses of the Earth in four and a half years.

Since the average adult red fox needs 5.7 pounds of food per week and a twelve-week-old pup needs about 4.8 pounds, a family of five consumes an average of 30.6 pounds of food per week. A meadow vole weighs about an ounce and a half, with 10.7 voles to the pound. When voles are numerous, foxes eat almost nothing else. That is to say, a minimum of 328 meadow voles per week — a rather conservative estimate — are needed to keep a family of five red foxes happy and healthy. To the farmer this is money, for 300 voles — with their rapid metabolism and nervous disposition — can crop grass almost as fast as a calf.

Two weeks later the foxes moved back to the sunny south-facing knoll and to the heart of vole country. Their third den, close to the crest, included a sweeping panorama of the river valley. In late May, when the pups were about ten weeks old, they began to explore the meadow and wooded hillside. At dusk they accompanied their parents on hunting forays, returning by dawn to bask in the sun like lazy farm dogs. Whether in the presence of people or red foxes, repose is contagious. So as the morning sun warmed the air, I rolled down my car windows, laid back in my seat, and nodded off.

10

ON FIRE ISLAND AND JONES BEACH:
A DANCE OF HAWKS

IT SELDOM RAINS in southwest Texas. Near the small town of Kermit, where austerity and the Llano Estacado (the Staked Plains) taper into the northern edge of the Chihuahuan desert, it is so dry that trucks deliver water twice a week. So dry that when it rains, cowboys say "a cow's pissing on a flat rock." Until I moved to Kermit as a graduate researcher, rain was rain. Then one afternoon as I combed the desert for coyote and bobcat scat, while the sky was still blue to the horizon, the ocean broke across my memory. Amid mesquite and juniper, badger holes and woodrat mounds, I abruptly sensed the pulse of waves, the soft ooze of marsh mud between my toes, and the stench of methane.

This strange backward sensation was both intimate and compelling. I felt myself on my father's shoulders, hanging onto his chin with all my might as waves broke across his chest. I had that eerie sensation of standing alone on the high board at the Jones Beach pool, looking down and wondering if I could go through with a dive. I saw myself peddling down the causeway, a kite tied to the handlebars and trailing in the wind. I watched as the kite snagged a wooden light pole and drove a marsh hawk from its perch, screaming high into the air. I heard Fowler's toads. I saw gray and white shorebirds wheel past the mud flats and orange and blue-gray kestrels hover, one after the other, above the rolling dunes. Although now restored and functioning as a navigational aid, the old Fire Island lighthouse, blemished by years of neglect, chaffed by a thousand ocean storms, and deserted and dark for decades, stood black and white before me as I felt the sting of a wet November wind.

Ocean-borne images swept over me, and by the time they faded there were rain clouds on the horizon. I knew for the first time that the pull of the ocean on me was so strong that I was imprinted like a salmon by the odors of my natal current, and that the very smell of water, fresh or salt, could release a wave of sweet memories.

Although Crest Road was too far from the shore for the sound of waves breaking, five miles more or less as the herring gull flew, invisible tendrils of salt air wisped through my neighborhood. There was always something happening by the ocean. It was a mecca for an incipient naturalist. I went there every chance I got. After getting my driver's license, I became a fixture along the barrier islands from Point Lookout to Democrat Point. That beautiful stretch of white beach with its waves and rolling dunes was a wild and wondrous zone, fragile yet enduring, and always changing. In late August the salt air bore a message, cool and crisp, that the barrier islands off the south shore — Jones Beach and Fire Island — were in a flux, and that autumn, hovering like a great osprey, was ready to descend.

I anticipated the fall hawk migration, for the sight of merlins and peregrines, osprey and marsh hawks, sharp-shins and kestrels passing over the barrier islands on an Indian-summer day unleashed a primordial magic. Hawks followed the cold fronts out of the lake states and New England, and with a northwest wind at their tails they poured down the Atlantic coastline. Their dance started in late August and ended by early November. Each year the steps differed, for the winds of autumn were fickle. But on a good hawk day I could almost feel the Earth cant.

I remember when, on a late September day near the old Fire Island lighthouse, a flight of more than five thousand hawks passed above the dunes and crossed the inlet to the eastern edge of Jones Beach. Some even abandoned land and cut across a tiny corner of the ocean toward New Jersey and Delaware. Birders much older than I called this the largest flight of hawks ever seen above the beaches of Long Island. After counting birds for an hour I gave up, leaving the task to more mathematical observers, and stood in rapt attention, waiting to be ordained beneath the pulsing river of feathers.

Using daily weather maps from *The New York Times* I taught myself to forecast good flight days by following the progress of an arctic cold front out of Canada, over the Great Lakes, and across Long Island. On the heels of the front came a couple of days of deep blue skies swept clean by gentle northwest winds that had crossed the sound, and neighborhood by neighborhood pushed southeast toward the ocean. Finally, two or three hours after sunrise, when the sand had warmed, columns of heated air rose high above the dunes and condensed into great fleeces of clouds. And below the clouds — hawks!

As I sat waiting in the hollow of a dune before dawn, a concourse of robins passed me and clouds of songbirds — warblers, vireos, flycatchers, sparrows — pitched into the belt of pine that ran west from the lighthouse toward the bay. The ebb and flow of these night migrants had ended. By sunrise hundreds of noisy flickers were everywhere. Soon the air and the sand began to warm, setting the whole beach in motion. Through binoculars, the distant dunes lost their shape as curtains of heat transformed them into dancing mounds of sand. Clouds scudded, white and soft. A loon appeared, then a long black arrow of cormorants shimmering like the distant dunes.

I scanned the horizon. Suddenly a kestrel, wings fluttering, rufous tail spread and arched toward the sand, hovered in the distance. Then another and another, and soon a line of these small orange and blue-gray falcons were strung on the wind east beyond the village of Kismet. A merlin cut past at fifty miles-per-hour to turn a hapless warbler into a rain of olive down. High overhead, an osprey. The dance had begun. A cluster of monarch butterflies, their wings freed of dew, unfurled and flew from a twisted red cedar. Soon they were everywhere. On the leeward side of the primary dunes, a line of monarchs passed within a hundred yards of the ocean. The butterflies flew low, rarely rising above the crest of the dunes. All day they moved, millions upon millions of them. Butterflies landed on my knees, my shoulders, and my head, pausing momentarily to stretch their wings (tickling me), then taking off for Mexico — a three-thousand-mile journey on guts and genes. They'd never return. Monarchs four or five generations removed from these southbound migrants would return to Long Island and everywhere else in the Northeast the following summer.

I came to know the participants of this annual pageant as one knows and anticipates the arrival of old friends. Merlin, for example, a surprisingly swift and pugnacious falcon slightly longer and more compact than a blue jay, with long, pointed wings and a long tail, delights in tormenting larger birds. I've watched them dart close to the pines to terrorize flickers, which bolted in every direction, squealing with the pain of surprise, then dart close to the bay, scattering large gatherings of black-bellied plovers across the mud flats. Once in a while a merlin would cut in from the line of primary dunes and pass me so closely that I felt the wind from his wing beats.

With my friend Richard Miller, an astute and athletic naturalist who subsequently became Long Island's first Tern Warden, I'd traipse down the beach looking for merlins, or squat in the big dunes by the Jones Beach garbage dump or on the roof of the old Smith Point pavilion and wait for sharp-shins and marsh hawks. For hours we'd talk about how lucky we were to have found companionship with nature, to be called back each autumn to this juncture of land and sea, to Walt Whitman's "endless inbound urge of waves." We rejoiced in the birds and wondered how people could pass the length of their days without the inspiration of sea, sand, and dancing hawks.

One October afternoon Richard and I stood with another friend at Point Lookout, commenting on the precision of peregrines and how wonderful it would be if one would fly over us, when at the height of our tributes a big slate-colored female sprinted overhead. We jumped into Richard's van and chased her for eight miles down

Lido Boulevard until the traffic thickened and we lost her. Another afternoon we broke up a basketball game to watch a half dozen kestrels being buoyed by the warm air rising off the blacktop.

As the sun set the parade of hawks and butterflies ebbed. Monarchs went to roost on the needles of red cedar and pitch pine. Some hawks settled down on branches, utility lines, and light poles; others pressed south. I left after the last visible merlin doglegged across the beach and disappeared into the darkness over the ocean.

If Fowler's toads anchored my boyhood, marsh hawks certainly buoyed my adolescence. They were the first hawks I ever met, the only hawks that regularly quartered the outer beaches of Long Island from Jamaica Bay to the Hamptons. Year after year they nested along the Jones Beach strip, at Tobay, Gilgo, and Cedar beaches, and if conditions were right — there being a bumper crop of meadow voles — they crossed the Great South Bay to nest in the marshes of Seaford and Massapequa.

Marsh hawks were a perfect introduction to the art of birding, as both sexes are extremely easy to recognize at a great distance. Females are larger, browner, and streaked below; males are gray above, with black-tipped wings, and cream white below. Thin, almost emaciated-looking, the marsh hawks would trace the contours of the dunes, their long wings held at a slight dihedral, their white rump patches bright even on cloudy days. Sometimes they'd hover. Sometimes they'd drift, buoyant and effortless as kites. With practice I began to recognize the young from the old, the first-year from the second-year birds. Yearlings of either sex looked like their mothers except for a rich russet bloom that extended over their breasts and bellies. During their second summer, after their first complete molt, young marsh hawks showed some signs of adult coloration; a dark patch under the wings separated them from the adult females.

Marsh hawks were the embodiment of all that was wild and lovely about Jones Beach, the very quintessence of the barrier islands. Although rare when compared with the astronomical number of herring and great black-backed gulls that crowded the coastal skies, I could always find a marsh hawk drifting over the dunes or perched on a wooden light pole. Fall migration was a protracted affair for the marsh hawks. Yearlings arrived before school started, were joined in mid-September by females, and replaced in mid-October by males. This sequence, triggered by the slanting sun, was as dependable as the arrival of Labor Day. Although there was considerable overlap in the length of their respective migratory seasons, the skies of August and early September belonged to yearlings, those of November to adult males. On that late September day when more than five thousand hawks passed over Fire Island, more than three hundred were marsh hawks — mostly young and female. By the end of Thanksgiving Day vacation, their passage over the outer beaches had ended, and those that remained stayed for the winter.

If the winter was mild and the meadow vole populations high, the marsh hawks were common and often could be found roosting in small aggregations. If conditions were harsh only a few hardy birds stayed, mostly males, while the rest moved southeast to volplane above the salt marshes of the Chesapeake Bay and the outer beaches of the Carolinas. Some even reached the sawgrass prairies of the Everglades.

I never call a marsh hawk a "northern harrier." No matter how much the American Ornithological Union (AOU) enjoins me to accept their official nomenclature, a marsh hawk is a marsh hawk, and will always be a marsh hawk. When I saw my first one in the early 1960s, nobody called them harriers. Our regional bird book, John Bull's classic *Birds of the New York Area* (1964), listed them as "marsh hawks." So did Roger Tory Peterson's third edition of *A Field Guide to the Birds*, although he stated that his preference was for "northern harrier." By 1974, the name "northern harrier" had gained ground. In Bull's *Birds of New York State*, published that year, the species account was titled: "Northern Harrier; Marsh Hawk," but in the text, they were still called "marsh hawks." The 1980 edition of Peterson's field guide stuck to the AOU's recommendation and called the birds "northern harriers," with "marsh hawk" relegated to parentheses.

The word *harrier* emerged in sixteenth-century England from the word *harien*, a military term that meant "to pillage and torment."

It is now the standard English name for all thirteen species of hawks in the genus *Circus*. The North American marsh hawk, *Circus cyaneus hudsonius*, a subspecies of the Eurasian hen harrier, was the only member of its tribe to have crossed the Bering Strait land bridge. When the AOU conformed to British usage and declared "harrier" our bird's common name, the modifier *hen* was dropped. Too many negative connotations, AOU officials insisted. Because the hawk ranges across the top of the world, *northern* replaced *hen*. "Northern harrier," a beige, lifeless name, was thus substituted for the color and poetry of a colloquial name, a name that conveys an immediate sense of place.

I will forever associate marsh hawks with miles of waving phragmites, salt marshes, and sand dunes. They are the birds of my youth, a symbol of my coming of age as a naturalist, and whenever I spot one — above the tundra, the Everglades, the desert of southwest Texas, the coast of California, or the hay fields of Vermont — I'm ushered back to the salt air and rolling dunes of Jones Beach.

In early April the hawks divided the marshes, dunes, and thickets into breeding territories. Gray males were rare, outnumbered six or seven to one (during migration the ratio was closer to fifty to one) by the yearlings and adult females. Usually two males worked the entire stretch of Jones Beach, seventeen miles of restless, shifting sand. Years later I learned that marsh hawks engaged in polygamy, not an uncommon trait among species of grassland birds. In these uniform habitats, food is concentrated in a small area close to the ground, and when the vole population is high — every three to five years — a single male can provide enough food for two and sometimes three families. During one high-vole year, Frances Hamerstrom (who studied the hawks for twenty-seven years in Wisconsin) found that immature male marsh hawks, the brown yearlings, bred upon entering their second spring, another reason why gray males are so outnumbered. So dependant are marsh hawks on voles that Hamerstrom gave her book *Harrier Hawk of the Marshes* the subtitle *The Hawk That Is Ruled by a Mouse*. She even speculates that microflora in the vole's gut may act as an aphrodisiac, playing a possible role in the hawk's fecundity.

Each spring I watched their courtship flights from the wooden observation tower at the John F. Kennedy Wildlife Sanctuary and from the mounds of bulldozed garbage at the Jones Beach dump. Sometimes I caught their action from the corner of my eye while driving down the causeway. I remember one gray hawk wheeling, fluttering, rising, and falling, always crying *kee-kee-kee-kee*. He'd stall a hundred feet above the sand, then with wings extended swoop down, *whooshing* through the air. Just above the briars he'd break, round out the dive, and bounce back into the air. Again he'd stall, then repeat the entire process.

When courtship ended, both marsh hawks gathered grasses and sticks. She built the nest. He continued to deliver building material and food. The grasses and sticks he brought directly to the construction site, but most of the food, after giving a sharp scream, he dropped. Alerted, she'd fly up, roll over, and pluck the morsel — usually a vole — out of the air and disappear into the briars. A quixotic mate, he did all of the hunting during the twenty-eight-day incubation, most of it while the chicks were confined to the nest. A female marsh hawk may have as many as seven young. If a gray male has two families, he hunts continuously from dawn to dusk.

I've never found a marsh hawk nest, although I've looked hard. Richard Miller and I would stand a quarter of a mile apart, each with a clear view of the poison ivy thickets, and try to "triangulate" on the male as he released food. Finding Captain Kidd's buried treasure might have been easier, for marsh hawks nest on the ground, walled in by a thorny and itchy vegetation. My worst cases of poison ivy followed these nest hunts.

While working on his master's thesis Richard spent three summers in the marshes of Cedar Beach and found that marsh hawks ate other things besides voles. They stole entire seaside and sharp-tailed sparrow nests, he said, taking the nest and chicks in one trip, and sometimes ate adult fish crows and glossy ibises. Even snowy egrets were taken. I've seen marsh hawks over the common tern colony on Jones Beach's West End. The terns would rise from the sand, hot-tempered and screaming, swarming the hawk and escorting it beyond the edge of their colony. Black skimmers, phlegmatic relatives of the terns, nested in the middle or on the edge of the West End colony and benefited from the terns' spirited defense. Only rarely did a marsh hawk slip through the terns' aggressive net and leave with a skimmer or common tern chick.

Because the grasses are dense and difficult to see into, a marsh hawk hunts owl-like, with its ears as well as its eyes. Its slightly dished-in face collects and amplifies sound. Any high-pitched mousy noise stops the hawk in midflight, and it hovers face to the ground before dropping with lightning speed, its long, nearly featherless legs and talons outstretched. If the hawk misses, it is up in an instant with legs extended, listening. Over and over it drops, rises, and listens until the vole is either caught or escapes.

Whenever I flushed a short-eared owl from its repose in the swales, a marsh hawk invariably spotted the owl, and a duel would begin. An owl-and-hawk dogfight is a spectacle to see. One bird outclimbs the other and dives with its talons extended. The lower bird rolls over and presents its own talons, forcing the attacker to break its dive at the last moment. Six or seven times the roles reverse, until the owl peels off and returns to its roost, and the hawk quarters down the beach. I never saw a winner or a loser, not even a ruffled feather.

Like marsh hawks, short-eared owls prefer open country, where they often winter in small communal roosts. Every three to five years, when the beach teemed with voles, a few short-eared owls stayed to breed. During those rare summers, the owls' encounters with marsh hawks were a regular event. In July 1979 Richard and I inadvertently found a short-eared owl nest while hunting for a marsh hawk nest. We saw a marsh hawk repeatedly swoop down on one spot until it flushed the owl. As both birds mounted the sky ladder, Richard and I walked through the salt marsh to the spot where the owl had flown from and found six young short-ears, gray balls of fluff with gleaming yellow eyes huddled against the frame of an old rowboat. We collected a bag of pellets, oblong packs of undigested food the owls had coughed up, and left.

I remember one cold January evening at the desolate eastern end of Fire Island an hour after the last marsh hawk went to roost. I huddled in the primary dunes, out of the bitter wind but within sight of the surf. To the west, toward the distant glow of New York City, the sky was a blackening orange crisscrossed with the soft vapor trails of jets. To the east, blackness. Two saw-whet owls appeared above the dunes like tiny puffs of smoke, and guided by the crashing surf and the stars of the northern hemisphere, headed west. Beyond them I saw a short-eared owl fluttering mothlike as it searched for mice. The following morning, a gray marsh hawk aroused the short-eared owl. Both combatants unleashed quick, but furious aerial assaults. First the hawk, then the owl rose into the frigid winter sky and dove, legs outstretched and talons extended. Once. Twice. Three times. After the marsh hawk's fourth dive, he left the owl and veered east over the dunes and swales of Smith Point, pushed onward by hunger.

II

GREAT HORNED OWL:
MASTER OF THE NIGHT

THE NUMBER ON the empty aluminum bird band read 792-54015. Judging from its diameter, the band had been placed on the leg of a songbird or maybe a tern, either a nestling or an adult caught in a mist net. The United States Fish and Wildlife Service issues bands to licensed ornithologists in an effort to individualize birds and record information about their life histories, in particular their migratory patterns. Sometimes the bands yield unexpected information.

Banding birds is easy. Recovering the bands is not. Less than 1 percent of all songbird bands have been returned. Naturalists waited several decades before a chimney swift's band came home to the American Museum of Natural History. The wintering ground of swifts remained a mystery until a team of anthropologists near the upper Amazon encountered Indians outfitted in bird-band jewelry. To the Indians, who had originally netted swifts for food, the shiny, malleable bands — undeniable gifts from heaven — were a sign of prosperity.

Band 792-54015, also a gift, was not acquired in the usual fashion — off the leg of a dead bird or one entangled in a mist net. And except for one interesting bit of natural history concerning the fate of a small bird, the secrets it revealed told more about my character than they did about the bird's. Well hidden, like a surprise in a Cracker Jack box, 792-54015 was bound in a knot of fur and feathers peeled from a short-eared owl pellet. In July 1979 Richard Miller and I had gathered more than fifty pellets by that Cedar Beach rowboat as six fluffy chicks spun their heads toward us to watch. Above us their mother dueled with a marsh hawk.

Pellets are indigestible tidbits, the remains of a predatory bird's dinner — fur, feathers, scales, bones, teeth, bills, claws and the chitinous exoskeletons of insects and crustaceans. Regurgitated instead of defecated, these dark, ovoid castings are full of secrets. Having relatively weak stomach acids, owls must return all of their prey's bones — leg bones, backbones, rib bones, and clean skulls with their grim smiles. Hawks on the other hand dissolve more bones, while herons, with their truly corrosive stomach acids, return only the ear bones of fish and the cheek teeth of rodents.

Earlier that summer, a short-eared owl glided over the marshes and dunes, heard a movement in the grass, and dropped in for the kill. It caught a small bird, swallowed it whole — an owl custom when feeding on small prey — and stored it in its crop, a saclike appendage that balloons out of the esophagus. When the owl returned to the rowboat, the bird passed out of the owl's crop and into the glandular segment of its stomach, the *proventriculus*, where peptic enzymes and hydrochloric acid began digestion. The little bird then passed to the muscular section of the stomach — the gizzard, or *ventriculus*. Feathers, bill, claws, and band separated from a now amorphous shape. A tiny opening between the gizzard and the small intestine drained the stomach.

In the gizzard, the little bird's feathers (and fur from a recent meadow-vole kill) wrapped around the little trophies; a pellet took shape. Cemented with mucus, it moved back into the proventriculus. Now the short-eared owl, as though suffering from bulimia, waited for hunger cramps to come, then threw up before eating. I've watched both barred and saw-whet owls do the same thing; they pitch forward, almost falling from their perches, then stretch out with their eyes shut and retch. Pellets help owls in two ways: they save energy by preventing the digestion of nonfoods, and when they are spit up they help scrub the bird's upper digestive tract in the same way that roughage cleans our intestines.

Pellets are treasures, gifts from a night bird that report on things I cannot see. I have often found the skull of a rodent or a shrew whose presence in an area was previously unknown to me. And fossilized owl pellets reveal Ice Age relations between predator, prey, and climate: lemmings in the hills of West Virginia; extinct rodents on the Galapagos Islands. I took the pellets to Vermont and stored them in the basement. Four and a half years later, having picked through hundreds of others, I gave a Montshire Museum student four pellets to examine. Along with the skulls of two short-tailed shrews, a least shrew, and six meadow voles, there was 792-54015, the most surprising item I have ever found in an owl pellet.

I mailed the band to the United States Fish and Wildlife Service's Bird Banding Laboratory in Laurel, Maryland. Three months later I received word that 792-54015 belonged to a common tern banded as a chick on June 17, 1979, in South Massapequa Park by Michael Gochfeld. Now Gochfeld knows his tern's fate (one of dozens he banded that summer) and that the short-eared owl pellet containing 792-54015 traveled to Vermont with an absent-minded naturalist who waited until more than four years later to pick through it.

Owls have always received mixed reviews from their human neighbors. When Pleistocene glaciers pushed the boundaries of the Arctic into central Europe, man met the snowy owl. In Trois Frères, in southwestern France, a chipped outline of a family of snowies decorates a Paleolithic cave wall. Later, charred bones recovered from Neolithic food caches show that the big white owls eventually moved from the foyer to the kitchen. Eskimos still eat owls, although Jews never did. The Book of Leviticus (chapter 11, verses 13–17) made it clear that owls — along with eagles, nighthawks, and cormorants — were not fit for human consumption. This biblical edict was based on the birds' habits, not on their palatability, although a biologist who ate a great horned owl assured me the meat was as tough and stringy as an old sneaker. That some owls reside in cemeteries, have loud, haunting voices, and do their work at night does little to improve their image. Owls now have their own public relations agents, naturalists, who issue the night birds' press releases. Each release is good, and each reveals a tribe of birds with a singular purpose: to ply the night currents in search of rodents and other small animals, an act beneficial to man.

Owls possess an array of physiological and anatomical adaptations that enables them to hunt at night. Among the more startling is virtually silent flight. Several things achieve this end: they have long, wide wings that support and spread their weight over comparatively large surface areas; the leading edge of their primary flight feathers is fringed and velvety soft, muting the sound of their wingbeats; and the owls' soft body feathers also help dampen sound as well as insulate against the weather. Even a three-pound great horned owl with a four- or five-foot wingspan — one of the most awesome predatory birds in the world — moves in and out of the shadows as silently as smoke.

Ears positioned at a different height on each side of the skull allow an owl to triangulate and pinpoint its prey across seemingly noiseless expanses. And those funny facial disks amplify and direct sound into the ears like parabolic cable-TV antennas. Laboratory experiments have shown that even sightless barn owls can locate and catch rustling mice. Allen Eckert, in his treatise *Owls of North America*, claims that some species "can hear the footfalls of beetles in the grass at distances of over one hundred yards, and the squeak of a mouse for a half mile." These magnificent auditory receivers work in concert with eyes that are just as remarkable.

Soulful and haunting, an owl's forward-looking eyes dominate its face. Their enormous size gives the bird a wise yet almost childlike appearance. Thick, long, and tubular, with huge round lenses and broad, light-gathering corneas, the eyes project bright images (even in dim light) across massive screenlike retinas that span the breadth of the bird's skull. Each lens is operated by striated rather than smooth muscles, which allow for a rapid and voluntary change of focus. An owl's tubular eyes are unable to roll back and forth, severely reducing its peripheral vision. To compensate for this narrow field of view,

it can rotate its head up to 270 degrees, often so quickly that it appears to be spinning in circles. These incredible light-gathering organs, uninhibited by daylight, are one hundred times more sensitive to dim light than our own. On a cloudy, moonless night when the woods are dark as a coal mine, the night reveals itself with unimagined clarity. A horned owl sees every twig on every branch in his path.

I stood with a friend in the crown of a seventy-foot hemlock in Dutchess County, New York. At that height the trunk narrowed to two inches, each branch to an inch, and when the wind blew the tree creaked. My hands squeezed the trunk as I looked across the canopy of the forest toward a slow, brown, weed-choked river. Two hundred yards from the hemlock, six crows swirled like a black storm, vocal and violent, through the branches of a large white pine. Inside sat their prince of darkness, a great horned owl. They hated the owl, and the owl's nest that was out there somewhere protected from the March wind by a wall of dull green needles. The crows knew where to find it, and each morning they tormented the owls. Sometimes blue jays joined them, and together the birds fed each other's fear and rage, a vigilant but powerless mob whose mortal enemy just sat like death and watched. For a month I had listened to the owls' amorous notes rip the night — deep, eerie duets that were less emphatic and less rhythmic than the barred owl's. The male's four low-pitched hoots lazily reached across the darkness; her hoots were higher pitched, more numerous, and dominated the night. Both chilled the crows.

Horned owls nest early, a month before the peepers stir. They refuse to build, preferring to steal their homes instead. With the snow still high in the woods, they lay two or three round, white eggs, often in a red-tailed hawk's nest. Lacking a hawk's nest, horned owls make do. I have found them nesting in a pocket of a west Texas sandstone cliff, in a crow's nest along the Bronx River, on a railroad trestle over the Connecticut River, and in a Long Island night heron's nest lulled by the surf. They lay eggs in squirrels' nests, in the cavities of old sycamores, and along the ledges of the Palisades on the Hudson River. On a remote New Hampshire beaver pond, I found one incubating in an abandoned great blue heron's nest. And once while in Florida I read about a pair of horned owls that shared a bald eagle's nest: an owl in one corner, an eagle in another.

Horned owls kill with bone-crushing power. With their razor-sharp talons, four to a foot, each an inch to an inch and a half long, they spear their prey. (Of the North American raptors, only the eagles have larger feet, longer talons, and a more powerful grip.) Once when a friend from Pennsylvania brought a hand-raised owl to a school — a routine he had performed a couple of hundred times — the horned owl suddenly tightened its grip, setting all eight talons in his arm. He left the school, the owl fastened to his arm, and drove to the nearest hospital. The bird had to be anesthetized before its talons could be prized from his arm.

From small birds to hawks and herons, from mice to skunks, nothing is safe from great horned owls. The Dutchess County birds trailed their shadows over less than a square mile of woods, fields, and marshes. Where one territory ended, the next began. Horned owls are cosmopolitan. They patrol the length of the Western Hemisphere from the tree limit in the far North, east and west from the city parks of New York and Los Angeles, and south through prairies, deserts, swamps, and tropical jungles, all the way to the Strait of Magellan.

The male sat in the white pine, his yellow eyes fixed on the crows. His mate hunkered on a platform of sticks across the forked branch of another pine forty feet above the ground and nine feet from the trunk. Beneath her were two white, fluffy chicks, protected from the elements and from the crows. Two other tree-top naturalists near-by spied an owl gliding through the stout branches of a pine and directed my attention toward the tree. As I awaited my next instruction, an owl flew out on soft, silent wings. Up there, hidden by a sweep of needles, was the owl's nest. For the first twenty feet the pine was branchless. To reach the nest we scaled a small beech tree then swung to the pine, thirty feet above the ground. I was terrified at first. One of the naturalists, an intrepid climber with a sense of security, tied an old hemp mountaineering rope to the pine so I could swing to the nest tree without turning pea green. In the days and weeks that followed I never approached the Flying Wallenda stage, but I did learn to accept the climb. My owl-tree ascents eventually developed into a regular morning ritual.

The chicks were young. Their thirty-six-day incubation began with the first egg, laid two days earlier than the second. The older chick was much larger than its sibling and had a dense coat of white down, as well as the strength to lift and rotate its head. The smaller chick, a mix of white down and pink skin, leaned its big, round head against the nest. The nest was littered with eggshells, and each chick still had its eggtooth, a white calcified point on the upper bill that helped free it from its shell. On March 25, about twelve days after the first chick hatched, the eggteeth were gone.

Each morning I combed the woods for pellets and other leavings. If the owls enjoyed good hunting the night before, two or three headless rats (the head is considered a delicacy, and the body is discarded when there is abundant prey) hung from branches or lay on the ground. The unused protein attracted other visitors. A gray fox scavenged whatever fell out of the trees. Fox scat filled with scraps of rats and rabbits — the two mammals that kept the owls fat and healthy — littered the area. Opossum and raccoon also passed regularly beneath the nest tree. Less than twenty yards from the pine an old, peeling sycamore with thick, broken stubs and long, serpentine roots was a favorite roost for the owls. I never actually saw them there — by dawn they were sheltered behind a screen of green needles — but most mornings a pellet or two lay by the sycamore's roots, and a thick, pasty whitewash stained its trunk or dripped from a low limb.

Keeping tabs on the owls' prey was like assembling a "who's who" for the woodlots of Dutchess County. Besides the rats and rabbits, gray squirrels, short-tailed shrews, least shrews, an eastern mole, and three species of mice — meadow voles, white-footed mice, and house mice — appeared in the pellets. One night an owl nailed a mink on a pane of ice that jutted out into the slow, weedy river. A dab of blood, a tuft of fur, and a lustrous brown tail marked the spot. I could imagine the scene as a diorama at the American Museum of Natural History:

Twilight, Dutchess County, New York. East lies Connecticut. Early April. Mackerel sky. Half moon with gilded clouds. Naked maples and somber oaks, dark hemlocks crowd the foreground. Two deer by the river. In blue-gray haze, a great horned owl — the main theme — rising from a shelf of river ice. A limp mink in its talons. Its mate in a grim pine, waiting. Twilight, eastern New York.

Nothing was too trivial for the owls: spotted salamanders on their way to vernal pools, beetles, crickets, and moths. Suckers gathered in the shallows to breed, their backs thrashing above the surface, provoked the owls. Twice I found the hind ends of large white suckers below the nest. Next to mammals the horned owls preferred birds. They were my guide to spring migration. Three days before I heard a woodcock, I found mottled brown wings and a knitting-needle bill in the nest. Flickers and a blue-winged teal showed up first in the nest then on my bird list. One morning I found the chicks sitting on a half-eaten ruffed grouse.

A male grouse makes an inviting target for a horned owl. Sexually hungry males drum from logs and stumps, boulders, and old stonewalls. Plump and full of energy, they vigorously pump their wings, feet planted firmly on their drumming post. Since owls hunt with their ears as well as their eyes, I wondered how male grouse survive their own breeding season. Every morning I heard them patter but found it difficult to pinpoint their location. The sound of the grouse's beating wings, low and directionless like the roll of distant thunder, comes from everywhere and nowhere at once. You feel it as much as hear it. I later read that great horned owls can do neither: tuned to the high-pitched twitter of rodents, they miss the Earth's low-frequency dialects. Unless an owl sees his performance, the drumming grouse is safe.

The chicks were well-fed; scraps of their orgies littered the nest. I even found snake scales in one pellet. Horned owls eat snakes, including timber rattlesnakes. (A Pennsylvania biologist once tracked the beeps of a radio-banded rattlesnake into the crown of a chestnut oak, a very unlikely spot for a rattlesnake. A day or two later, a beeping radio was found in a coughed-up pellet at the base of the tree.) The chicks grew with the urgency of spring rising with the sap. The larger they grew, the more the nest shrank. At four weeks they were half-grown, the nest half-gone. At six weeks the nest was so abused that the larger chick had slipped through to perch on a pine limb ten feet below. At dusk it climbed parrotlike up the trunk and back to the nest limb.

A horned owl's face pulls you toward its yellow eyes. Framed between large ear tufts — the "horns," which are used in nonverbal communication and have nothing to do with hearing — a white throat bib, and the dark brown edge of the facial disks, they look like two glowing embers. It is a beautiful face, one that belies the owl's ferocious nature. And the horned owl trains those haunting eyes on formidable prey: fox pups, young raccoons, house cats, and weasels. Last winter a friend found a dying horned owl impaled on porcupine quills. And some biologists speculate that a fisher's avoidance of meadows and frozen lakes may be an avoidance of great horned owls.

Horned owls kill boldly marked, slow-moving skunks. The owls lack a sense of smell, and unless they are temporarily blinded by the spray, skunks don't have a chance. In the winter of 1984 near George's Pond in Enfield Center, New Hampshire, I jumped an owl which dropped a big, warm skunk. Some ornithologists claim they can locate the owls by the odor of skunk wafting down from trees. I've handled owl skins that still smelled of skunk after years of storage in museum drawers.

Among birds, only eagles and big herons are safe from horned owls, which douse the fire in the eyes of hawks — red-tailed, red-shouldered, marsh, Cooper's, and sharp-shinned. Even peregrine falcons are killed at night on their ledges. Barred, barn, long-eared, and screech owls, among others, turn up in the horned owl's nest. American bitterns, too, and Canada geese. Crows are also a delicacy. The crows know this, and their blood fairly boils at the sight of a horned owl. Three or four times a day crows mobbed the nest site in Dutchess County, screaming their distinctive, powerless war cry. I heard crows from across the river — jagged and shrill — first one, then another, until the sky roiled with their noisy confrontation. The crows fell silent in April, however, when they became busy with their own nests.

The horned owls slept in peace then. But at twilight they evened the score. Predictable and defenseless, crows sat by their nests. Black eddies of feathers drifted beneath the sycamore, the pine, and along one of the woodland trails. And the crows never forgot.

After the first few visits to the nest, I searched the literature and found several rather gruesome accounts of naturalists who stayed too long or too close to nesting great horned owls. There is this note by A.C. Bent in his *Life History of North American Birds of Prey,* Part Two:

> Once, when I was not looking, I felt the swoop of powerful wings, then a terrific blow on my shoulder, almost knocking me out of the tree, and I could feel the sharp claws strike through my clothes. . . . As I neared the nest, I felt a stunning blow behind my ear, which nearly dazed me, and off sailed my hat a hundred feet away; her sharp talons had struck into my scalp, making two ugly wounds, from which blood flowed freely. This was the limit; I did not care to be scalped, or knocked senseless to the ground, so I came down. . . .

Charles Keyes, writing in 1911 for *The Condor,* described an owl attack that ripped open his left cheek. Another report told of a great horned owl that opened three deep gashes four inches long across a biologist's arm as its mate attacked from behind. But the strangest great horned owl story I've heard was told to me by Bob Atkins of Ely, Vermont. One cold winter evening, as Atkins and his wife sat down to supper, a starving owl arrived unexpectedly for dinner. Mistaking the back of Atkins' head for a small mammal, it crashed through the double-pane storm window in the dining room. Fifteen minutes later the owl returned, burst through the inside window and bounced off Atkins' head, opening several shallow scalp wounds. After several laps around the house, Atkins snagged the owl in a fishnet and gave it to the raptor rehabilitation clinic at the Vermont Institute of Natural Science.

On April 27 both chicks, now nearly full grown, left the pine and settled on the ground. Their nest was gone, worn-out. The owlets couldn't fly, but that didn't matter. With their adult-sized legs and razor-sharp talons they could lie on their backs with their feet facing the opposition. No fox, raccoon, or naturalist would bother them. The next night, as the sun set behind the Taconic Range, I crouched in the bushes and watched a silhouetted horned owl carrying a limp mammal in its talons drift through the woods, noiseless as a cloud. When it landed on the ground by the pine, the owlets caterwauled — wild, frenzied screams that I imagined seared the crows.

As spring wildflowers bloomed and faded and the warblers arrived to breed, the young owls ranged farther afield. By the second week of June they flew. Again the parent owls' peace of mind was in jeopardy. Now, when the parents returned with prey, the owlets chased them to the roost tree and begged. And begged for most of the summer, attaining independence at the end.

Last December, after the sun passed below Emma's Hill and the gray winter twilight began to gather above the Connecticut River, I spotted a large bird perched near the top of an elm fifty yards from the northbound lane of Interstate 91 in North Hartland. I thought the bird was a red-tailed hawk; it was certainly big enough. As I drove closer, I noticed a large round head sitting squarely on neckless shoulders. Then I noticed the ear tufts. It was a great horned owl, my first horned owl sighting in the Connecticut Valley in more than six years. I swerved the car into the bird-watchers' lane and hastily backed up. Perhaps the owl didn't think much of my driving, because it leaned forward, unfurled its great wings, and rose into the twilight. One flap. Two flaps. Three flaps. Each easy and noiseless like the soft swish of a feather duster. Away it went across the snow-covered pasture toward the brooding wall of cottonwoods and silver maples that keep the river company.

12

THE WILDER DAM EAGLE

THE WHISTLE HIT A SINGLE NOTE, loud and long, and sent it straight up like an arrow. Thirty-four bands of dyed porcupine quills, flattened and woven together in tight alternating triangles, colored the whistle's stem red and yellow. Two plumes from a big bird, perhaps an eagle, hung from one end. Strips of sinew bound the quills to the bone, and soft, white leather from an antelope or a mule deer bound the feathers and looped around the mouthpiece so the user could hang the whistle from his neck. Behind the shrill note, forming a delicate counterpoint, was the rhythmic pounding of a skin drum, a tom-tom: *BOOM, BOOM, BOOM, BOOM, boom, boom, boom, boom.*

Made of bone ceremoniously cut from the wing of a fallen eagle, the whistle had been used by Plains Indians to call upon the wind and the sun, upon the buffalo and the elk, upon their Grandfather the Great Spirit to guide them down the good road. Since the eagle flies the highest of all birds, he flies the closest to the sun. He sees the land curve toward the horizon, and he sees everything as one.

According to Sioux tradition, he is the solar bird and his feathers are rays of light. His voice, so piercing, strikes both the earth and the firmament, indeed the center of the universe, awakening the Great Spirit in the People. Within the bone whistle lives the voice of the eagle, and the voice of the Great Spirit, for they are one.

Bone whistles were made from the large wing bone of a bald or golden eagle — the bone which anchors the tendons and flight muscles of the sternum. Since the bone is hollow, converting it into a whistle was easy. A Holy Man cut a quarter-inch half-circle a third of the way up the stem, then fit a tiny piece of wood, clay, or resin with one side sloping up into the hole, so that air forced through the mouthpiece rode up the sloped fret and out the hole. The piercing, primordial sound compels attention. This whistle, which was given to Dartmouth College along with a collection of other Indian artifacts by an Oklahoma alumnus, was in cold storage at Wilson Hall, pending identification and a catalogue number. Greg Schwartz, the Assistant Curator of Anthropology at the college's Hood Museum, needed a hand in identifying the feathers and fur that decorated some of the artifacts, so Linny and I stopped by to help, and to make some music.

As I fingered the bone whistle I had visions of the Sweat Lodge and Sun Dance, of white buffaloes and big birds. After a few moments I gave the whistle a cautious toot, just enough movement to sway the feathers at the end of the stem. I did it again, softly so as not to arouse the spirits or disturb the curator. Linny began tapping the taut head of a skin drum. Two more toots. Silence. And then, with reckless abandon, I blew out a century of dust from inside the bone. Greg gracefully accepted our musical digression. The shrill voice of the whistle raced up my spine as Linny drummed and smiled. She knew my thoughts had drifted to the eagle.

I had seen the big bird on Friday, high above Wilder Dam. With wings flat and his primary flight feathers extended, he circled the edge of a thermal, head and tail white, body and wings brown. Around and around, with eyes that resolved eight times more detail than my own, the bald eagle saw the whole of the Upper Valley: two states, one watershed. From his sky perch he looked down the

Connecticut to where the White River, the Mascoma, and the Ottauquechee brought their water, to where the Connecticut grew white
and restless at Sumner's Falls. Upriver toward Hanover and Norwich, he saw Mink Brook, Blood Brook, and the Ompompanoosuc,
the tower of Baker Library shining in the sun and the snowcapped
summit of Mount Moosilauke. He saw the hills with their knobby
peaks — Gile in Norwich, Smarts and Holts in Lyme, Cube in Or-
ford, Cardigan in Canaan — like rippling water that gently rolled
away from the Connecticut toward the mountains, green and white.

The eagle saw everything: the farms, the condos, the sewage-
treatment plants, and all the plumes of wood smoke that rose from
the valley. He saw the ribbons of asphalt that stretched like big black
snakes from Connecticut and Massachusetts, and endless lines of cars,
skis and poles fastened to their roofs. He saw the bus station and
the train station in White River Junction; the airport in West
Lebanon.

I blew louder and longer upon the bone whistle.

Wilder Dam will never be the same. No longer will I think of
the open water, black against the ice, as just another riverine attraction for winter ducks, common mergansers, and common goldeneyes
or as just another source of winter mist. The eagle changed all that.
I first saw the big bird during the winter of 1981. He was perched
in the elms and cottonwoods that flank the Connecticut River below
the mouth of the Ottauquechee. His back lit by the afternoon sun,
he sat in the company of several hundred crows. The crows buck
winter by mining undigested corn and insect larvae from manure
mounds along River Road in Plainfield, and in April they spread
through the valley to breed. But the eagle, a rambler from parts
unknown, an immature bird that found the river to his liking, stayed
for a few days and then disappeared as mysteriously as he had arrived.

The following January an eagle returned to the elms in North
Hartland and fished Sumner's Falls a mile or so downriver. After
bunking for a week with the crows, he moved north six miles to
Wilder Dam. He stayed until ice-out, and since then an eagle has
returned to the dam every winter for seven years in a row. I cannot

be sure whether each winter I watched the same eagle set up housekeeping behind the dam, diving for suckers and walleyes and mergansers, or whether each year the roost trees and open water lure a new bird that ekes out a living alone in the wilderness. I can speculate, though, for bald eagles have progressive molts. Year by year the dark brown yearlings gradually achieve their distinctive adult plumage, which is attained during their fourth or fifth year.

Between its first and fourth year, an immature eagle becomes more mottled with white, particularly on the belly, underwings, and tail. In 1981 the immature bird in North Hartland was quite dark, with some flecks of white or buff below. A year later the visiting eagle had a much lighter lower breast and belly, mottled with dark, and a distinctive dark hood that extended down over the upper breast like the yoke of a sweater. In 1983 the bird was lighter still, with big buff patches on the breast, belly, underwings, and tail. And in 1984 a near-adult with wisps of brown on its white head and along its outer tail feathers had settled in for the winter. On January 20, 1985, an adult bald eagle arrived at Wilder Dam, left after seven weeks, and returned on December 6. It was gone by March and back on December 20, 1986.

For a bald eagle to live along this or any stretch of the Connecticut River, the entire watershed must be clean. For it depends on the absence of pesticides, DDT in particular, in order to survive. The river was not always so clean, nor were eagles always so healthy. Bald eagles held their own during the urbanization of the East Coast, breeding in scattered colonies from Newfoundland to Florida Bay and inland along the bigger rivers and lakes. But by the late 1940s, something had gone wrong. In 1939 Paul Muller, a Swiss chemist, developed a chlorinated hydrocarbon called DDT while tinkering in his lab. Muller was given a Nobel Prize for his work; the eagle, osprey, and peregrine falcon received a death sentence.

DDT sprayed on farm land and forest, shade trees and ornamental shrubs washed into the river and collected in the flesh of fish, crippling their nervous systems. The bigger the fish the more its body absorbed. As eagles consumed the moribund fish, quantities of DDT entered their own bodies and were stored in their fat. Each spring female eagles burn their fat reserves to provide the energy necessary for migration, nest building, and egg laying. As the fat was broken down, DDT was released into the circulatory system and accumulated in the shell gland, inhibiting the synthesis of calcium carbonate. Thin-shelled eggs resulted, eggs that could not support the weight of the incubating female.

Bald eagle nests produced fewer and fewer young birds. The last pair to nest in New Hampshire disappeared from the wild shores of Lake Umbagog in 1949. The old white pine nest tree, straight and tall like a flag, still stands, empty and forlorn. Wintering eagles, like the Wilder Dam bird, became scarce. During most of the 1950s, evidence was building up against DDT. Researchers in the upper Midwest were convinced the pesticide was at the heart of the problem. Their data from Michigan, Wisconsin, and Minnesota confirmed it, for dead and dying birds — robins, marsh hawks, and eagles — had large concentrations of DDT in their fat deposits and brains. But where was the evidence from the Northeast?

During a dinner party in the winter of 1963, a Hanover matron complained to Charles and Doris Wurster of the Dartmouth College Biology Department and Medical School that robins went into convulsions and died each spring on Hanover's lawns. She suspected DDT was to blame, for every April the town sprayed their beloved elms to control the spread of Dutch elm disease. The Wursters, both biochemists, agreed to look into the situation. For three nights, beginning April 15, 1963, approximately 1,285 pounds of DDT — about half a pound per tree — were sprayed on more than two thousand Hanover elms. Norwich, then not nearly as affluent as Hanover, could not afford to treat its elms. The Wursters thus had a control population of birds, one that was almost free of DDT, that could be compared to the contaminated Hanover population: a perfect set up for a scientific experiment.

The Wursters and two friends surveyed a fifteen-acre section of Hanover and an ecologically similar section of Norwich. Robin counts were made on their way to work from 7:00 A.M. to 8:00 A.M. and at lunch. The counters traded routes daily from April 8 to mid-May, so as not to bias the results. After mid-May the counts were spaced at intervals of two and three days until mid-June. The results were so striking that the study has become a seminal piece of work, a primary thread in the development of the Environmental Defense Fund, one of the leading private watchdog organizations against environmental abuse.

Nothing happened the morning after spraying the elms. It took weeks for the DDT to travel from the trees into the soil and into the earthworms. By mid-May, dead robins and robins with tremors, diddling and fluttering as though victims of Saint Vitus' dance, began to appear in Hanover. Although Norwich had a few dead robins, none had tremors and none had lethal dosages of DDT in their tissues. All the Hanover casualties were contaminated with fatal levels of the insidious pesticide. And the chemical did not stop with robins. Swift and lethal, it reached not only earthworms but also bark and aerial insects. Chipping sparrows, yellow-rumped warblers (which were just passing through town), tree swallows, and bark feeders — white-breasted and red-breasted nuthatches, yellow-shafted flickers, yellow-bellied sapsuckers, downy and hairy woodpeckers — were also infected.

Hanover lost more than 70 percent of its breeding robins in 1963, and Norwich, relatively free of the effects of the pesticide, actually gained a few birds from nearby floating populations. Of course, not everyone was convinced by the results of the study. One California scientist claimed that the robins had simply flown across the river, thereby explaining the population decline in Hanover and the slight rise in Norwich. But dead birds don't fly. The ground crew at Dartmouth College heeded the Wursters' warning and switched to a nontoxic pesticide, methoxychlor, in 1964. Although there were still a few dead robins that spring, the result of residual DDT, the population rebounded and there was no evidence of the poison in other bird species.

The Wursters split up. Doris stayed in Hanover and Charles left for the State University of New York at Stony Brook, Long Island, where he continued what he had started in Hanover, and became recognized as a world authority on the toxic effects of DDT. At his insistence, Suffolk County, Long Island, became the first

municipality to ban the pesticide. With a few colleagues he formed
the Environmental Defense Fund and in 1972 brought about the
ban of DDT in the United States. It all started in Hanover, with
a few dead robins and a casual study conducted on the way to work.
For this the Wilder Dam eagle should be thankful, for his river is
clean once again.

Not everyone appreciates eagles. Benjamin Franklin thought the
bald eagle was low and despicable, a dastardly bird that stole fish
from ospreys, scavenged with gulls, and whose voice, a harsh, cackling
kak-kak-kak-kak-kak, was more like a chicken's than a noble bird
of prey's. Franklin lobbied for the wild turkey as the national symbol. Fortunately, no one listened.

I saw my first bald eagle above an Adirondack lake, soaring high
against a cobalt sky. I've seen them in the cottonwoods along the
Snake River in Grand Teton National Park, above the Everglades
and tidewater Georgia, over the sand dunes of Long Island, above
the Kittatinny Ridge of eastern Pennsylvania, and close to the city
limits of Miami, Los Angeles, and the District of Columbia. I've seen
them in every season — breeding, wintering, and migrating. I've
watched bald eagles from my car, from a blind, while hiking, walking, and jogging, from canoes and kayaks, and from a twin-engine
Otter and a Cessna 2000. Wherever people tread lightly, eagles fly.
And when a bald eagle arrives unexpectedly, its presence is a cause
for celebration. In June 1977 an immature bald eagle showed up at
the Manchester Sanitary Landfill in southeastern New Hampshire.
The event was reported in the *Manchester Union Leader* and the *Concord Monitor*, attracting scores of people to the pines above the dump.
Whenever the eagle swooped into view, chasing a pigeon or a herring
gull or a rat, the bird got a standing ovation.

After years of progress in pollution control, the Androscoggin
River, which flows out of the northwest corner of Lake Umbagog
and goes through Berlin and Gorham before veering east into Maine,
was reclassified by the New Hampshire Water Supply and Pollution Control Commission. Now the river is considered safe not only
for swimming and fishing but also, to the delight of North Country

residents, for bald eagles. During the winter of 1980 a pair of eagles — a large, immature female and a smaller, mature male sporting full adult plumage — roosted on a hill behind a shopping plaza overlooking the Androscoggin. The river bank teemed with sightseers. I queried the Gorham police about the whereabouts of the big birds, for I thought they would know of any uncommon gathering of people. They did. I was directed north on Route 16, a mile beyond a power company dam, to the parking lot adjacent to the river. There, beneath a warm, cloudless sky more typical of July than February, a crowd had assembled.

I stood with my back to the river for an hour as the eagles sat high in a big white pine above Rich's Department Store. Then the immature female, the more aggressive of the two, chased her companion into the air. He flew directly over our heads and began circling. Cars pulled off Route 16 and kids on bicycles skidded into the gravel parking lot. The eagle soared higher. Twenty-seven people watched, many with binoculars in hand, focusing and refocusing. A patrol car pulled up, not to disperse the crowd but to join it. John Scarinza was off duty but still in uniform, on his way home from the night shift. He checked the eagles four or five times a day, he said. He was their self-appointed guardian, their most devoted observer. John knew the eagles. He could predict when the birds would leave their night roost, when they'd hunt, when they'd fly, when they'd perch. He also knew the eagle watchers. "In all," he told me, "half of this town and part of Berlin, Milan, and Randolph have parked here to see the eagles."

The female (who is always the larger of the two sexes) left her roost and joined the male. Both eagles flew back and forth not ten feet above the Androscoggin, trailing their shadows over the river as dozens of common mergansers, which were what had kept the birds in Gorham, scattered like leaves each time the eagles passed overhead. All day the eagles stayed, and all day the spectators came. By late afternoon I had counted more than one hundred people. Some had come for the first time. One car full of women who had heard rumors about the birds at the laundromat timed their visit to coincide with the drying cycle. Next door to the parking lot the men at the St. Johnsbury trucking depot took a break, crammed their cheeks with tobacco, and joined us in the parking lot. And shoppers traveling north to Berlin detoured around the parking lot, took a look at the eagles, then headed north to market.

I returned the following weekend to find the eagles still there, the weather warmer, and the crowds bigger. I met three men, each of whom claimed to be the first person in Gorham to have spotted the eagles and each with a story to back up his claim. They postured in the morning sun as though playing *I've Got A Secret*, casting aspersions upon the credibility of their competition. The eagles still soared, pinned to the wind. By midafternoon the parking lot took on the aspect of a street fair, and Route 16 that of a field of bumper cars, drivers advancing and stopping, one eye on the road, one on the sky.

The Wilder Dam eagle has never been that predictable. Other than breakfasting on fish trapped in the shallows, and frequently perching in a red oak or paper birch, the bald eagle patrols the Upper Valley from Lyme south to North Hartland, and west up the White River to take Atlantic salmon from the Federal Fish Hatchery in Bethel. A Norwich farmer lost a pinioned Canada goose to the big bird, and in Hartford the eagle visits the back forty to clean up sheep guts. A comptroller at the Lebanon Airport picked up the eagle on radar, soaring fifteen hundred feet above the river. And he is no stranger to the West Lebanon and Hartford town dumps. Everywhere the eagle goes, he draws an audience.

I look for the bald eagle in the gray light of dawn just before Wilder Dam discharges water, when he leaves his red oak perch and drops, talons extended, toward the shallow pools. One morning he leaped four times from the oak, dipping toward the water with wings extended and raised slightly above the horizontal. His tail angled down, shifting from side to side like a rudder, and his feet trailed below like landing gear. The passes were casual, not those pushed by hunger, just broad, lazy arcs down from the oak, over the ducks, and across the river. The mergansers never moved.

After the fourth pass the eagle flew to a silver maple on an island half a mile below the dam. While he was gone, I walked down to the red oak and found the remains of suckers and a walleye. There was no sign of a duck carcass, but some electricians with the New England Power and Electric Company told me that when Wilder Dam held back water the eagle harassed the mergansers, which bunched together and waited for the big bird to thin their ranks. But for the most part fish were the eagle's lodestone, suckers mostly, and he never gave 'em an even break.

Boston is a thirsty city. In order to quench its thirst, the 1927 Massachusetts legislature decided to take the Swift River valley and create the Quabbin Reservoir, the largest man-made domestic water supply in the world. Before the valleys of the east, west, and middle branches of the Swift were flooded, 4 little towns — Enfield, Dana, Prescott, and Greenwich — had to go, so 650 houses, 2,500 people, 7,561 bodies from 34 cemeteries and a bunch of cows were relocated. Now all of metropolitan Boston, more than 40 cities and towns with more than 2.5 million people, depend on the Quabbin. So do bald eagles. By flooding the Swift River valley, the Metropolitan District Commission also created, as one writer phrased it, an "accidental wilderness." With 181 miles of shoreline and 39 square miles of water surface with limited access, the Quabbin Reservoir became a winter home to both the largest gathering of bald eagles — 41 were reported in 1986 — and bald-eagle watchers in the Northeast.

Thousands of people visit the Quabbin each winter. In 1982, when the Massachusetts Department of Fish and Wildlife needed to know how the eagles contributed to human visitation, I wrote a public survey which my New England College Endangered Species class administered at random to visitors parked at Quabbin's Enfield Lookout. The results showed that on average each car brought 3 people, traveled 27.5 miles from home, and visited the reservoir 17 times each winter; 59 percent of the people came to watch eagles, 36 percent came for the scenery, 4.6 percent had no particular reason for being there, and 0.4 percent were lost.

The first wintering bald eagle arrives at the Quabbin in late November. More show up as arctic air shuts down the lakes and marshes in eastern Canada, and by the middle of March the number of big birds that loiter on the reservoir's pine-studded islands peaks.

Eagle watchers follow the same pattern. Locals visit the Quabbin all winter, but in early February many of the cars parked along the dike and scenic overlook are from elsewhere in New England. Last February I met a vanload of New Yorkers who drove up for the afternoon, a woman from Virginia, and a pack of Cub Scouts from western Connecticut. On days when the sun is bright and the wind brisk, the overlook is filled with cars and the sky with eagles.

Quabbin eagles are carrion feeders. White-tailed deer brought down by dogs or coyotes and road kills left by state biologists keep the eagles well-fed all winter. So crowded is the reservoir with dead deer that I once saw seven carcasses on the ice, five with attendant eagles. One morning, while several of my students watched in rapt horror, three golden retrievers chased a doe onto the ice, disemboweled her, and left. Within an hour an immature bald eagle settled onto the steaming meat.

With this in mind, I lobbied the Vermont Fish and Wildlife Department for a deer carcass to lure the Wilder Dam eagle into better view. I didn't have to wait long. The next morning Bob Rooks brought over a yearling doe, solid as stone, that had been bashed by a tractor-trailer. We tied the deer to a toboggan, strapped on snowshoes, and lumbered down to the Connecticut a couple of hundred yards below the dam. After staking the carcass into the snow, Bob wired on a note that read, "Do Not Remove. This deer belongs to the State of Vermont." The note made no difference. A dam employee told me that a fisherman walked out to the carcass, looked it over, then shoved it downstream. The loss of the deer was mine, not the eagle's. With so much open water below the dam and at Sumner's Falls, the big bird had access to fish, and if he developed a craving for red meat, someone somewhere in the valley was sure to have butchered a sheep or calf and scattered the offal. I lost a chance to lure the eagle into the open, to keep him on the ice morning after morning, so the people of the Upper Valley could come to the dam to pay it homage.

Every autumn more than twenty thousand eagles leave the hinterlands of Canada and move south across the face of North

America. Eagles from the prairie provinces follow hordes of waterfowl, a movable feast, out of the marshes and potholes, spreading south and west from Lake Michigan to the front range of the Rocky Mountains. Along the Pacific Coast they attend salmon runs, gathering by the thousands near Haines, Alaska, and in lesser numbers down the coast to northern California. In New Mexico and Arizona, bald eagles hunt jackrabbits, often in pairs, and in Montana and Idaho, when the landlocked Kokanee salmon introduced by state fish and game departments move upstream to spawn, eagles are there.

In the East bald eagles visit national wildlife refuges to dine on crippled waterfowl, catch alewives and eels at low tide, and are regulars at hydroelectric plants where turbines grind up fish and hold back ice. Tennessee Valley Authority projects support eagles, as do large municipal water supplies and the mouths of big rivers like the Merrimack, Hudson, Susquehanna, and the Potomac. Migrant and wintering bald eagles arrive in November and are gone by April, and although they mate for life they often spend the winter apart. Southern bald eagles reverse this cycle. They court in November, nest in December. Once their young are self-sufficient, they head north with the sun to loaf in the pines and spruce that fringe blue glacial lakes. These eagles are random opportunists and may appear anywhere in the North Country.

I've seen an adult bald eagle summering on Lake Umbagog for the past seven years, and every now and then one works the lower end of the White River near Sharon and West Hartford. At the Willard Pond Wildlife Sanctuary in southern New Hampshire during the summer of 1976, I watched a pair of loons, a day-old chick wedged between them, rise up with bills pointed like bayonets toward the sky and wings spread, ranting and raving. Above them, an adult bald eagle changed its mind, broke its dive, and swerved away, disappearing into the morning mist. The following summer, seventy miles farther north, an eagle flew past my window while I spoke on the telephone. But by August and September, while northern eagles still tend their young, the southern birds turn around, tails to the North Country, and head home.

Southern bald eagles lead an easy life. At land's end in the Everglades National Park, where the coastal prairie fades into Florida Bay and mangrove islands called keys sprout in shallow estuarian waters, fifty-seven pairs of eagles nest. When the tide's high they fish for mullet, but when it's low eagles go after the birds — herons, egrets, gulls, even pelicans — that gather in extraordinary numbers on the marl flats. I found the wing of an egret hanging like a badge from one eagle's nest, and beneath others I found the bones and feathers of herons and cormorants. And no matter what the tide, an osprey with its catch is never safe.

One morning as I sat alone on the edge of Florida Bay, an osprey caught a mullet and struggled to get it aloft. Before the fish hawk was ten feet off the water, an eagle appeared and stooped with half-open wings, talons extended. The osprey dodged its attacker once, twice. But the mullet slowed it down. As the osprey filled the air with cries of distress the eagle, silent, resolute, and with a fire in its eye, dove again. This time the mullet fell. Lighter, the osprey rose screaming into the blue vault of the Florida sky. The mullet hit the earth alive and flopping, less than twenty feet from where I sat, and the eagle, without the slightest bit of hesitation, plunged and lifted the fish aloft in its talons. Off toward a key went the big bird with her prize;, the osprey followed at a distance its *kree* of protest ringing out across the bay.

Each winter a group of bald eagles convenes in the Catskill Mountains of southeastern New York. A series of three reservoirs — Swinging Bridge, Mongaup Falls and Rio — which were built on the lower half of the Mongaup River to generate hydroelectric power in the 1920s and 1930s keep open water below the dams all winter. Eagles like this, and they like the dead and injured fish that pass through the turbines.

I learned in 1975 that except for state biologists and members of the Sullivan County Audubon Society, few people paid attention to the Catskill eagles. One morning I drove to Monticello, took a motel room, and continued south for fourteen miles to Forestburg, a tiny bedroom community for the Orange and Rockland Utilities

Corporation, the company that owns and maintains the reservoirs. From Forestburg I drove west several miles to a bridge over the Mongaup River. There I waited, but saw no eagles. I waited longer. Finally, cold and bored and not at all sure I was in the right spot, I took the river road south, hoping to meet someone who knew where the eagles were. The road wound through a stand of old-growth hemlock and sugar maple, where rhododendrons curled their leaves against the cold. Across the river I saw no houses, just big woods running from the bank, up and over the horizon. This was primitive country, one of New York's best-kept secrets.

About five or six miles downriver I found a boat ramp and a sign that warned "Trespassers Beware." A quarter-mile beyond that was the only house for miles around, a two-story cape that faced the water. The ramp, the sign, and the cape belonged to the Orange and Rockland Utilities Corporation, as did most the land on either side of the lower Mongaup. I took my chances. I parked by the ramp and slipped into the woods, following the shoreline north for more than a mile. There were no eagles here either, but I did see a couple of ice shanties on the far side of Rio Reservoir. Without a second thought, I headed for the fishermen. Surely they had seen eagles. A hundred yards from the shore, the ice gave away and I was treading water, binoculars in my hand and a field guide in my pocket.

I attempted a series of muscle-ups, as though performing on the high bar, but each time I pushed up the ice fractured. I kept pushing until I left a trail toward the shore like a miniature ice breaker. Finally I reached a stiff shelf of ice, did a muscle-up, and slid forward, afraid to stand. I moved snakelike across the ice, spread-eagled to support my weight. When I hit land, I grieved for my binoculars and my original field guide, then ran like crazy for the van. Warm and sweating, I reached it in a minor state of shock only to find the van was stuck in mud. Without help, I wasn't going anywhere.

Gene Raponi watches bald eagles. He works for the Orange and Rockland Utilities Corporation and lives in the cape down the road from the boat ramp. He is the caretaker for the utility company's land. He dislikes people who don't read signs, who wander onto private property and fall through the ice. He and his sons were the only people around, and my only source of help. After he thoroughly ragged me, we humped the van back onto the road, and I headed off to the motel to thaw out. The following weekend, warmer and dryer, I returned to the Mongaup. Eagles were everywhere, and close. They passed over the bridge in groups of three and four, played on the thermals high in the March sky, and sat like statues in the giant riverine pines. Two immature birds hopped about on the frozen river, picking and scratching at chunks of fish imbedded in the ice. At sunset, the eagles went to roost on southwest-facing ledges, high above an old railroad trestle and out of the wind. At sunrise, they returned.

In 1980 I brought my endangered species class to the Mongaup. We reached the bridge at dawn. The sky was gray, the ice was gray, and the little fox chipping at the frozen deer on the river was also gray. At the first sign of color in the sky, an immature bald eagle flew in from downriver and perched in a nearby white pine. The fox lost its appetite and slunk back to the shoreline, throwing glances over its shoulder. The eagle never flinched. Moments after the fox disappeared, a pair of crows landed on the ice fifty feet from the carcass. For crows, the eagle had no patience. He bolted his pine and settled by the carcass, forcing the crows back. They kept their distance, hopping and fluttering and cawing, as the triumphant eagle stood like a monarch on the ice.

An hour after sunrise five bald eagles gathered, four adults to feed on the deer, and the immature, less like a monarch and more like a serf, to wait with the crows. As the adults jostled for position the crows slipped in for a quick bite. The immature eagle, half hopping, half fluttering, tentatively worked his way toward the carcass. He didn't get too far. A big adult female threw out her wings, flapped twice, and the young bird froze. All morning the party grew — more eagles, more crows — as the carcass shrunk. By early afternoon the eagles and crows were sated and my students were exhausted and hungry, so we broke for lunch. Afterwards we drove north to Roundout Reservoir, another hydroelectric project. Where turbines kept the water open below the generating plant, several hundred ducks gathered — mallards, blacks, lesser scaups, ring-necks, common goldeneyes, common mergansers — as well as dozens of herring and ring-billed gulls. And on the ice at the water's edge, a duck crumbled in his talons, stood the shepherd by his flock.

When we returned to the lower Mongaup, we stopped to see Gene Raponi. Gene was in the front yard, his wife was hanging wash in the back. I thanked God he didn't recognize me. He enjoyed our tales of the eagles, the gray fox, and the waterfowl. He was pleased, too, that we came all the way from northern New England to enjoy the big birds that he so loved. He told us about a woodchuck that bluffed an immature eagle into giving up its attack and about an adult bird that snagged a Canada goose after a brief, spirited chase. For more than an hour Gene entertained us with eyewitness accounts of the eagles and the people who came to watch them. He saved his most condemning story for last. The class already knew the punch lines and the points of action. I had told them about my troubles with the ice and mud as part of their orientation to the Mongaup eagles. As he began, they looked at me, laughing. I had no choice but to confess my identity. Gene, blushing and bewildered, stared at me for a moment then yelled to his wife, "Honey, the idiot's back."

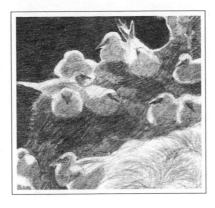

13

OF PUFFINS AND PETRELS

THE WIND CHURNED AND PLOWED THE SEA, pushing up five-foot waves that slapped the sides of the lobster boat. I held on to the cabin and bent my knees to hold my position on the greasy deck. It was futile. My sea legs failed and my constant shuffling amused the reticent old lobsterman. When a sooty shearwater scaled past, I released the cabin, fumbled with my binoculars, and slid rather quickly toward the stern. Returning to the bow, I toiled forward, grabbing lobster pots and plastic drums like a commuter working through a crowded, rocking subway.

It was 4:30 A.M. The sun was still below the horizon, and lavenders and pinks freshened the eastern sky. In the distance gray fog knitted gray ocean to gray horizon. A crescent moon hung in the west, fading. I was on my way to Machias Seal Island, twenty-five acres of rocks and seabirds in the mouth of the Bay of Fundy, nine miles east of Cutler, Maine. Within an hour the sun revealed the island and the lines of seabirds that streamed out of it like rays of light. By the time the birds passed us their lines had splintered into bands of twos and threes. Terns, buoyant and graceful, elevated flight to an art, darting above the swells on the long, thin wings that carried them in winter to the very edge of the planetary biosphere, to the Antarctic ice floes. By contrast, puffins, stiff and awkward, teetered on the threshold of flightlessness. They veered left and right, constantly fanning their small wings, as otherwise they'd fall into the water. Puffins are compact birds, with tiny humming wings that pump four hundred times per minute and carry them up to sixty miles per hour. But rather than rise above the waves, they cut through them like a band saw.

Terns were obstreperous, puffins silent. As we reached the shoals the chatter of terns rose above the noise of the surf and the whir of our engine, as they proclaimed the height of the nesting season. Machias Seal Island had no dock, so the lobster boat dropped anchor one hundred yards from shore. A marine biologist with the Canadian Fish and Wildlife Service picked me up in a dory and ferried me toward a half-submerged scrap of metal that he called a boat ramp. The ride to the island was an adventure, up swells, down troughs, through splashing whitecaps; I felt as though I was in a Winslow Homer painting without my fisherman slickers. Everything I brought with me — cameras and lenses, tripod, film, and paper — was wrapped in plastic bags. The lighthouse keeper, who moved as deftly on the slippery algae-covered ramp as a purple sandpiper on jetty rocks, escorted me onto Machias Seal Island.

Although it lies five miles closer to the Maine coast, Machias Seal Island is claimed by both the United States and Canada. The rich fishing grounds around the island keep its ownership in dispute. The United States owned Machias Seal Island before 1820, the year Maine gained statehood, but left the jumble of rocks and its attendant birds to the gray north Atlantic and the whalers who wasted the rookeries for meat. After losing several ships on its covetous shoals, England erected a lighthouse there in the middle of the last century to guide her interests into the Bay of Fundy. America didn't seem to care.

Canada inherited the lighthouse from England in order to protect her own ships. On navigational charts New Brunswick includes Machias Seal Island even though the United States Coast Guard patrols the surrounding water and Maine fishermen dredge scallops and trap lobster offshore. The ongoing dispute has not been without incident. In 1974 Barna Norton, owner and captain of the Audubon Queen, the only licensed tour boat that visited (and still visits) the island from Maine, complained to his state senators that Canada had restricted visitation and his tour business had suffered. When a U.S. Coast Guard cutter chaperoned the Audubon Queen to Machias Seal Island, the Americans were received by a military helicopter from New Brunswick. Still unresolved, the dispute sits in international court.

After orienting me to the island, the biologist and the lighthouse keeper returned to work. Two wooden blinds with sliding wooden shutters stood on glacial granite above the western shore. Between the blinds and a narrow trail that circled the island, a belt of tall meadow grass danced in the wind. Unlike common terns, which nest in the open, arctic terns prefer tall grasses. This zone was theirs. Passing through it was no different from passing through a common tern colony. When it comes to nest-site protection, a tern is a tern.

They rioted. A squadron of arctics rose from their nests, screaming and shitting long plumes of white, chalky stuff that hung in the air for a moment before covering me with streaks. Two or three dove at my head, jabbing me with belligerent red bills. I shielded my eyes. Now several dozen — a maelstrom — swooped and screamed, *keer, keer, keer, keer, keer*, voices firing like automatic weapons. When I entered the blind and shut the door, the terns lost interest.

The rocks belonged to the puffins, which had fled silently over the water when I opened the blind. On their return they stood upright and stared at the blind, a gawking crowd of comical birds. The puffins, portly and penguinlike, moved with a swagger, scuttling about on bright orange legs. White on front, black on back, with black neck bands and enormous triangular bills — blue at the base, red at the apex, with a yellow rosette in each corner — they made me think of a parade of tiny W.C. Fieldses in formal attire, replete with bow ties and light-bulb noses.

Their mouth linings flashed a deep yellow-orange when they yawned, gaping yawns that made them appear as though they were engaged in conversation. Whenever a puffin landed, others rushed to it, waddling and bumping, fluttering stubby wings, intent on minding each other's business. Then they yawned long ritual yawns that somehow bore the stamp of individuality much like fox urine or finger prints. Puffins are great divers. They enter the water while floating and propelled by short, stiff wings reach depths of up to three hundred feet. When they surface, slender fish dangle crosswise like silver whiskers from their bills. I counted nine in one bill, seven in another (the record is twenty-eight). Because puffin bills are serrated, each fish stays in place wedged in one behind the other while more are collected. After the breeding season the outer covering of the bill, flame red and steel blue, is shed, leaving a smaller, yellow bill.

Behind the puffins stood the dignitaries of Machias Seal Island, razorbill auks. Razorbills dressed like tuxedoed diplomats — black above, white below. More sedentary and less inquisitive than puffins, they ignored their neighbors' business and stood flat-footed and fixed: a rather phlegmatic bunch. Razorbills lay a single tapering brown-blotched egg that blends into the guano- and lichen-stained rocks. The narrow end of the egg is heavier, so that if kicked it rotates in a tight circle in one place. Puffins dig burrows and lay a single white oval egg. They occasionally lay a dark egg, a throwback to a time when they competed for rock space with the razorbills and had to camouflage their eggs from marauding gulls.

Puffins, razorbills, and other members of the family Alcidae — dovekies, common and thick-billed murres, and black guillemots — were once so abundant they covered the north Atlantic like an immense oil slick. Relentless slaughter by Europeans and colonists for meat, eggs, feathers, fat, and bait crippled the colonies. Great auks, large, flightless alcids, disappeared so quickly that for years their existence was thought to have been a myth. By 1830 they survived on only two islands off Iceland. Volcanic eruptions sank one island that year, limiting auks to Eldey Island. Fishermen finished them off, taking fifteen in 1830, twenty-four in 1831, thirteen in 1833, nine in 1834 and three in 1840. On June 3, 1844, three Icelanders on a collection mission for a Danish museum strangled the Earth's last two great auks and smashed their pear-shaped egg.

Gone was the north Atlantic's only flightless seabird. A great black and white bird, a product of gray, foggy seas and gray, foggy islands, it had wintered off the Grand Banks of Newfoundland, occasionally swimming the length of the continent to Florida and back like a humpbacked whale. A dig on Funk Island thirty miles east of Newfoundland uncovered piles of great auk bones, attesting to the regular visits whalers and sealers paid to the rookeries. From that dig the Montshire Museum acquired a composite auk skeleton more valuable than a Stradivarius. Skins are rarer. And stuffed auks should qualify as World Heritage Sites. I've seen just one, at Harvard's Museum of Comparative Zoology. Another was auctioned off for $33,000 at Sotheby's in 1971.

Puffins suffered, too. By 1900 they were limited to two islands in the Gulf of Maine: Machias Seal and Matinicus. Maine responded by passing the Model Wild Bird Act in 1901. In 1916, representatives of Great Britain and the United States formed an international agreement to protect migratory birds passing through Canada and the United States. On July 3, 1918, President Woodrow Wilson signed the Migratory Bird Treaty Act, and the two governments began regulating seasons and prohibiting the sale, purchase, or taking of migratory birds or their parts.

Some birds fared better than others. Arctic terns repopulated offshore islands that had been silent and idle for decades. Puffins, birds of immutable habits, prospered north of the international border. Before they could repopulate islands in the Gulf of Maine, puffins needed help. Since 1973 more than eight hundred chicks — one ornithologist said they looked like something that came out of a vacuum cleaner bag — have traveled from Great Island, Newfoundland, to Eastern Egg Rock in Muscongus Bay. In 1981 five pairs of puffins nested for the first time in almost a century on Eastern Egg Rock.

For six hours I lived in the blind, watching the sun arc above Machias Seal, basting the rocks and seabirds with warm, yellow light. But the sea, furrowed and whitecapped, grew restless. By noon small-craft warnings had been posted and island tours were cancelled. The lobsterman returned, moored offshore, and radioed the lighthouse keeper to tell him that I'd be stranded if I didn't leave immediately. I packed up, moved gingerly through the terns' aggressive net, then negotiated the slippery and now movable boat ramp. The keeper and the biologist steadied the dory as I stepped over the gunwale. Twice, swells drove us against the rocks, heaving the dory as though it was a toy. All three of us turned the boat and shoved off, half hopping and half skipping, one foot in surf, the other in the hull.

The ride to the lobster boat was choppy and wet, and filled with tension. I hugged my camera gear. To change boats required some proficiency in gymnastics, for the dory pitched forward and back and up and down with each swell. Safely aboard, I stood and watched the lighthouse keeper and the biologist struggle back, then capsize thirty feet from shore. The fisherman laughed a deep, hearty laugh as though he hadn't experienced anything so amusing in years. In no position to laugh myself, I remained reverent and thankful that my camera gear was safe. By the time we unmoored the keeper and the biologist had reached the metal boat ramp, the dory submerged at their feet. I helped the lobsterman haul traps and sort his catch. We reached Buck's Harbor amid a roll of eight-foot swells and fading daylight. As the darkness thickened I drove up the coast, attentive every now and then to Machias Seal's pulse of light flickering across the night.

Quebec's Gaspé Peninsula juts into the Gulf of St. Lawrence north of New Brunswick. On the eastern end of the peninsula lies the village of Percé, a haven for fishermen and tourists. Two miles east of Percé lies an eighteen-hundred-acre island of red sandstone and conglomerate, a relic of the Carboniferous period. It is roughly egg-shaped, with 250-foot sheer cliffs blanketed with white spruce and balsam fir, and on its edges dwell noisy seabirds. Every year Bonaventure Island gets a little smaller, eroded by the tidal gulf.

After leaving the lobsterman in Buck's Harbor, I crossed New Brunswick in the dark, reaching Percé shortly after 4:00 A.M. At 8:00 A.M. the first tour boat left Percé for Bonaventure. I was aboard it. The boat swung around the eastern end of the island, past cliffs white with gannets and black-legged kittiwakes, past colonies of common murres packed in crevices and crowded on ledges, past a handful of puffins, ledge-nesting razorbills, and a trio of harlequin ducks, adventerous waterfowl that prefer storm-racked coasts and turbulent mountain streams.

Squalls of white gannets, the island's main attraction, wheeled above the boat and the rose-brown sandstone cliffs. Tapered at both ends, with sulfur heads and white six-foot wings tipped extensively with black, the gannets scaled above the water or dove for fish from heights of up to one hundred feet. The murres watched, moving off the lower shelves whenever the tour boat passed too close.

A footpath crossed the island through spruce and fir to the edge of the gannet colony. Engrossed, I missed the last boat back to Percé. All day a blizzard of gannets sailed above the cliffs, flat wings translucent in the noon light. What grace they had in flight escaped them on the ground; like lummoxes, they shook and wagged and waddled, nipping at each other whenever one passed too close. An immature bald eagle twice came in from the mainland looking for unguarded chicks or chicks splattered on the rocks below, a posse of gannets and kittiwakes in close pursuit. After sunset the gannets settled down, and stranded without accommodations or equipment I joined them, reclining in the grass by a band of stunted white spruce.

All that afternoon I stood above a petrel colony, watching the domestic affairs of gannets, never suspecting that these tiny relatives of albatrosses and shearwaters hid in burrows beneath my feet. Petrels dig while lying on their sides, shoveling and kicking two- or three-foot tunnels into soft earth that is often shadowed by overhanging spruce. Some burrows are inherited; some recently dug. All are very hard to find.

Leach's storm petrels, pelagic wayfarers no bigger than a wood thrush, come ashore to breed on islands and rocky, desolate beaches on both sides of the north Atlantic and north Pacific. They are birds of boreal water and the night. During the day their honeycombed community is as still as stone. One parent waits at the end of each nest chamber with its solitary egg or young. It waits in darkness for its mate to return across a trackless ocean, a wait without food

that can last for up to four days. Chicks are fed only when a parent returns, and sometimes live without light for sixty days.

As darkness descended I heard a cooing, not the mournful cry of the dove but a more rhythmic, effervescent call that came from the sea and above the cliff, filling the night air with a queer, lighthearted laughter. I imagined elves or spirits ascending from the sea. Suddenly I saw them, petrels silhouetted in the moonlight, flitting erratically like moths or bats. I was on the top of a petrel colony. Too excited to sleep, I grabbed my flashlight and stalked the odd little birds. In and out of the light beam they flew, searching for their burrows. I walked to the base of a small spruce, sat down, and watched a petrel awkwardly settle on a limb close to the trunk. It hooted four times, left the tree, returned, and hooted again. Then an eerie sound rose from the ground, a soft murmur, liquid and long like a distant garbled voice. The tree bird hopped to the ground, entered its burrow, and the duet continued, muffled voices rolling out of the earth as though the sandstone itself were crooning. I listened to the duet for some time, my ear fixed to the ground, and wondered if these subterranean songs had spawned the Micmac Indians' fear of Bonaventure, a fear that kept them off the island. For the Micmacs, Bonaventure was plagued with an ogress, Gougou. I knew, too, that the sound of innocent little petrels terrified stranded mariners. For those still afloat, petrels were omens of ill fortune, the souls of drowned seamen. And because they nest on both sides of the north Atlantic, maybe, just maybe the tales of the Lilliputians of the British Isles had been spawned by the wails and twitters and purrs of petrels.

Leach's storm petrels can live for more than twenty years, an oddity among small birds, whose life spans are generally not more than three or four years. They come to land in June and lay an oversized white egg wreathed with lilac that hatches in forty-two days. The devoted petrel couple regurgitate oily food for their chick for two months, then the parents abandon the nest. The young petrel, now heavier than its parents, waits alone in the dark for several days living off a robe of fat. Hunger forces it out. Although raised without light next to an ocean it has only heard, the young petrel leaves the island abruptly for the open water. There it flits above swells, picking at small fish, mollusks, and crustacea and following whales, feeding on the oily globs that drip from their mouths. It sleeps on the water's surface.

Aware that Leach's storm petrels toil over northern oceans for nine whole months, taxonomists named them *Oceanodroma leucorhoa*, the white-rumped ocean wanderer. I've seen their white rumps from whale-watching vessels as the birds danced over the waves, but on this night I heard and saw only their magical voices and silhouettes.

By 2:30 A.M., the colony fell silent. The last moonlit petrel passed beyond the sandstone cliffs and headed toward the dark ocean well before the herring and great black-backed gulls awoke. The gulls drive Leach's storm petrels into the night. Above land or water, and even in bright moonlight, tireless gulls chase, catch, and swallow petrels whole. At midocean migrating peregrines, refueling en route to the neotropics, also catch them. By dawn clouds of gannets soared above the cliffs, while others scuttled about stealing seaweed and grasses from unguarded nests to add to their own. The first tour boat reached Bonaventure at 9:30 A.M. Fifteen people crossed the island looking for seabirds. Watching gannets and kittiwakes, they passed over the hidden, silent petrel colony.

14

PA·HAY·OKEE: RIVER OF GRASS

BY MID-FEBRUARY IN VERMONT male chickadees have begun to whistle their two-note *fee-bee, fee-bee*, and the sun sets after 5:30 P.M., but I am ready for more than a subtle promise of spring. I need more than a day trip to Plum Island on the northeastern Massachusetts coast to rekindle my spirits; I need to knock a month off the Vermont winter. I need a tropical coast away from bitter winds and bright snow, from temperamental cars and icy roads. I need Florida and the Everglades.

My parents sold their Long Island home in 1983 and moved to Brooksville, Florida, coincidentally and conveniently only twenty miles south of Homosassa, where Linny's dad lived, and thirty miles south of the Crystal River. We'd visit both our families, then in the morning, when my parents were ready to play golf at the Seven Rivers Country Club, we'd drop them off, launch our canoe, and spend a day with the Crystal River manatees, Florida's largest wintering herd.

On one of our visits we rented a plane. The sun rose above the cabbage palms and the short, wide river. Both scuba diving and fishing tours had not yet marked the river with flotillas of Boston whalers, motorized rowboats, pontoons and houseboats, and large motorboats. In my mind I erased Route 19 as though it was an oblique parenthetical phrase. Gone were the hotels, the marinas, the commercial strip with its Ronald McDonald playground, the shoreline houses, the docks, the billboards advertising cheap land and new communities. From my perch in the Cessna I focused on the length of Crystal River, from its headwaters in the limestone springs of King's Bay to six and a half miles downstream where it empties into the Gulf of Mexico. I saw mounds of hydrilla, squadrons of nervous coots that roiled the surface, and patient herons scattered motionless along the shore.

From my turkey vulture's point of view eight hundred feet in the air, the manatees looked like gray slugs idling near the surface of the blue lagoon. Ponderous and languid. Three times we circled the bay to count them. Seven manatees attended one group, five another. Without rippling the water a mother and a calf swam slowly across a wide inlet, past bright orange buoys that marked the Banana Island Manatee Sanctuary, one of three sections of the Crystal River National Wildlife Refuge where boats and divers are not allowed. Linny and I counted a total of seventeen manatees; several were inside the sanctuaries, most were not. Swimming with manatees, I imagined, was the only way to truly appreciate them.

Early the following morning, after scraping a light frost off the windshield, Linny and I drove to the Crystal River and launched our canoe into King's Bay. A manatee almost as long as our boat passed under us, close enough to the surface for us to see the sunlight stroke its back, painting bright quavering checkerboards from its head to its tail. Caribbean sailors who knew no other lady except for the one on the bow of their ship often mistook the sensuous contours of manatees for the legendary mermaids; starvation, deprivation, and lots of rum worked hallucinatory wonders on the sailors. Manatees are square-headed and whiskered, sausage-shaped and fat, with fingernails on their flippers and a large, oval, horizontally flattened tail. Except for a pair of axillary nipples which might have struck the early explorers as small breasts, little about them suggests a woman. Christopher Columbus carried the myth to the New World, reporting mermaids off the coast of Haiti in 1493 that "weren't nearly as beautiful as painted." When the Spanish realized that manatees weren't mermaids, the church declared them to be fish, which made them available to Catholics on Fridays.

The West Indian manatee belongs to the order Sirenia, whose name was derived from Homer's seductive sirens by way of the Spanish *sirenias*, which means "mermaid." Sirens diverged eighty million years ago from the same stock of primitive mammals that spawned elephants. Unlike seals and walruses, manatees lean on land only to support their weight as they prune bank vegetation. They are up to twelve feet long and weigh as much as thirty-five hundred pounds. They give birth in the water to sixty-five pound calves, which nurse for up to two years, the strongest social bond a manatee has. Unlike cetaceans, however, manatees never developed the elaborate vocal communications associated with social hunters. They just squeak and rub each other a lot.

Sirens once contained more than twenty genera. Of the four species which survived into the twentieth century, three are manatees in the genus *Trichechus* — the Amazonian, the West African, the West Indian. The Indo-Pacific dugong is in a separate genus that bears its name. A fifth member of the order, Stellar's sea cow, a toothless, kelp-feeding giant from the Bering Sea, was exterminated by sealers and whalers in 1741, about a quarter of a century after its discovery. The West Indian manatee, which reaches its northern year-round limit in Florida (occasionally wandering in summer to coastal Texas and Virginia), swims the tepid waters of the Caribbean, the gulf coast of Mexico and Central America, south to the north coast of South America, and down to Brazil's Margue Seca.

Manatees are slow-moving vegetarians whose food is rooted and abundant. They stay close to the coast, going up warm rivers, seldom moving into deep oceanic water. When the air temperature dips below 50 degrees in winter, they bunch in the vicinity of springs and power plants like old men gathered in a steam bath and let a constant gush of warm water caress their large bodies. Many of the manatees I watched summered in White Water Bay in the Everglades National

Park and spent November to March in the Crystal River. When the air temperature rises above 70 degrees, manatees scatter from King's Bay and disperse throughout the length of the river. With an average daily discharge of 600 million gallons of water and a temperature that never falls below 74.6 degrees, the Crystal River attracts more than 120 manatees, about one-tenth the state's population.

Although Jacquin Sanders, an inspired *St. Petersburg Times* reporter, described a manatee as "a large blob, about the size, shape and color of an old Packard," his colleague Betty Kohlman called them "underwater teddy bears." She must have swam with them. Manatees are gentle, lovable creatures that sometimes delight in human company. Their continued existence is threatened, however, by the very creature with whom they fraternize — man. More than 80 percent of the state's 1,300 manatees have had their backs gouged by powerboats and between 30 and 40 of them die each year as a result of those collisions, even though the Florida Department of Natural Resources posts signs that read "Manatees, No Wake, 5 MPH" in critical rivers and bays.

I put on my wet suit, flippers, mask, and snorkel, grabbed my Nikonos, and jumped in. Much to my chagrin I discovered that swimming, snorkel-breathing, and photography were not innate functions driven soley by enthusiasm. But the friendliness of these huge creatures encouraged me to keep trying. I swam up to a manatee that idled about twenty feet from our canoe and began to scratch its head. Two black button eyes, set in folds of skin that looked like weathered rock, stared back at me. To be fondling an unassuming wild mammal ten times my weight was awesome. Its flippers, front limbs modified for swimming, gently sculled the water, sending eddies up to the surface. With a halfhearted twist, the manatee rolled over and exposed its belly. It wanted a stomach rub, spoiled no doubt by other people who swam here before me. I obliged. Five minutes later, having tired of the massage, the manatee drove gently forward, powered by its flattened tail.

I followed it along a path between dense entanglements of hydrilla that rose fifteen or twenty feet from the bottom like the walls of a canyon. A familiar aquarium plant native to north Africa, hydrilla escaped from the pet trade and has spread across Florida like a plague, choking rivers and lakes. Schools of mullet grazed the hydrilla, moving through the dense waving branches. Using its prehensile upper lip to grip the plant the manatee assumed a posture of prayer and stuffed vegetation into its mouth with both flippers. I swam closer, to less than a foot from its face. I watched it chew, abrading the plant's cellulose frames with its large molars. From the corners of the manatee's mouth bits of crushed food leaked out and rose toward the surface like green smoke.

Linny joined me and we snorkeled around King's Bay. We found a manatee asleep — they can stay twenty minutes under water — on the sandy bottom, its nostril flaps shut tight, its back propeller-scarred. Another rubbed against our anchor line, flaking off old skin, exoparasites, and algae. We watched a double-crested cormorant break the surface. Silver bubbles streamed from its black feathers as it chased a small fish. Schools of mullet and big yellow- and turquoise-colored jacks flashed past. A fourth manatee, resting at the water's surface in morning sunlight, sponsored three zebra-striped fish that picked at the fuzzy growth of algae covering its back. We swam to it. Through our masks and with snorkels in our mouths, Linny and I smiled broadly as we spun the manatee, rubbing and scratching its firm sides. It rubbed its head against Linny's stomach: interspecies communication. A ten-foot, two-thousand-pound marine mammal that enjoyed our company. It was, as Linny said afterward, "a very close encounter."

From Brooksville, Linny and I drove south toward the twenty-four-hundred-square-mile Big Cypress Preserve and the Everglades. The cold snap that had brought manatees to the warm springs in King's Bay had swept thousands of tree swallows south from the Carolinas. On Interstate 75, between Fort Myers and Naples, we passed below a ten-mile stretch of swallows— stragglers, small groups as well as enormous flocks that wheeled and dove from the cloud heads to the tree tops along the highway. From Naples we headed southeast on U.S. Route 41, the Tamiami Trail, passed beneath more clouds of tree swallows, saw an armadillo rooting for grubs, road squashed opossums and raccoons, and finally entered Big Cypress, the heart of Florida panther country.

In 1976 Florida biologists estimated that three hundred panthers, a southern race of mountain lion, still roamed southern Florida. By 1984 the estimate fell to thirty. Elementary school children voted the panther the state animal, and in 1982 the state legislature wrote it into law. Bright yellow road signs bearing stylized cats warning motorists to "Slow Down" and "Beware" were placed at critical wildlife crossings. Former governor Bob Graham demanded federal highway funds for the construction of forty animal underpasses along the 76.3-mile Alligator Alley, called by biologists "the road-kill capital of the world," where the final leg of Interstate 75 is scheduled to go all the way from Naples east to Miami. Still, each year three or four panthers are walloped by trucks. One road sign had read "Less Than 30 Remaining," but was now corrected with spray-paint to read "28." Two more panthers had been killed. I stopped by the sign and studied the traffic. No one slowed down; two cars even sped up when they saw me.

From Alligator Alley we drove south on State Road 29. More panther signs, more speeding motorists. Off State Road 29 north of Copeland was the Fahkahatchee Strand State Preserve, twenty-five miles long and seven miles wide, 44,538 acres of wilderness panther habitat that lies between the Big Cypress Preserve and Collier-Seminole State Park. The strand, land bordered by two obscure rivers that water Big Cypress, is considered by naturalists to be the panthers' most critical habitat.

As we motored along the narrow graveled W.J. Janes Scenic Drive, anticipating a Florida panther, we reviewed the results of an informal epiphyte census conducted by University of Florida biologists on the branches of the strand's towering trees. On six trees, between one thousand and ten thousand orchids and ten thousand to one hundred thousand bromeliads grew. A barred owl passed silently in front of the car as Linny read aloud from a reference book. Then suddenly the rutted, pot-holed Scenic Drive ended at a paved two-lane road. According to one of our references, the road, penetrating like an arrow through a limb of this swampy wilderness but going nowhere, had a name: SW 98th Avenue.

There was no SW 97th or 99th Avenue, and as far as we could tell, SW 98th Avenue was the only paved road available to the turtles and snakes of the Fahkahatchee Strand. The road had been built in the late 1950s to "improve" an otherwise miasmic piece of real estate. A developer who sold improved lots with water to out-of-staters thought a paved road with an attractive numerical name would entice investors to splash their cash into this pristine south Florida wetland. The developer hoped that SW 98th Avenue would conjure images of a bustling city, of hot dogs and symphonies. That was the first step. Next, he planned to drain the swamp, divert the run-off of more than fifty inches of rain a year, log out the cypress and oaks, and clear out the worthless swamp-dwellers, the panthers and black bear, the armadillos, raccoons, cottontail, and deer. To hell with the orchids and gigantic royal palms. The Swamp god, however, took a dim view of the project. The scheme went belly-up, and the state bought the land, preserving a resource of irreplaceable value.

The sun set as we drove away from the strand. By the time we reached the Tamiami Trail it was black out, and for the moment darkness hid the canals and floodgates along the road — the scars of civilization. From the side of the road little eyes shone in our headlights, and when we opened the window we heard the frogs' choruses. State Road 94, an unimproved gravel road in the Big Cypress Preserve, loops back off the Tamiami Trail twenty-four miles to the Monroe Ranger Station, past ponds and sloughs and innumerable stands of dwarf cypress that are separated by the open water and the slash pines that grow on slightly higher ground. Moonlit Spanish moss festooned the trees like giant cobwebs and made the land appear wilder and more beautiful.

We headed for Jerry's RV Campground, a small and comfortable place with soft grass, electrical hookups, and hot showers in the middle of the wilderness seven miles down the jagged Loop Road. On the way we stopped to identify a DOR pig frog, a big green southern "bullfrog," whose grunting, hoglike voice blended with the resonant moans of southern leopard frogs and the clicks of southern cricket frogs. DOR opossum. DOR black racer, flattened and dried to a dark leather. Linny spotted a frog, alive and sitting in the road. Oops. In my delirium, I backed over it: DOR southern leopard frog, filled with eggs. We drove on.

Where the Loop Road twists south, we spied a tawny-colored bobcat, lighter and smaller than a New England cat. It ran down the road, not glancing back, pumping its thin legs. I followed, the bobcat in my high beams running twenty miles an hour. After a spirited several-hundred-yard chase that sent a rain of maps, books, and papers off the dashboard with each rut and pothole, I reluctantly slowed down. In the distance, at the farthest point of illumination, the cat slipped into the dark pines. I drove to the spot where it had veered off the road. We listened for fading footfalls, but heard only frogs.

We arrived at Jerry's RV twenty minutes later, set up a tent in a far corner behind an old chicken coop, ate a sandwich, then got back into the car and headed west on the Loop Road. The headlights struck an opossum. I slammed on the brakes, got out and ran after it. Off the road and into the cypress. Moonlight lit the opossum as it scrambled around in the woods. I cornered it. It bristled with defiance, flashed a wide, toothy grin, and hissed. No fainting. I grabbed it by its naked, prehensile tail and toted it back to the car, beaming at my own virility. Linny wasn't impressed. The headlights revealed the opossum was old and emaciated, with busted teeth, its eyes glazed with the blue haze of cataracts. We released it knowing that a bobcat or a panther or a 'gator would have an easy meal.

Farther down the road the ruts were so big and numerous that Linny drove as if eggs were on the bumper. All of the windows were open and amid grunting, honking, squeaking frogs we heard amorous notes from a pair of barred owls: *hoohoo-hoohoo, hoohoo-hoohooaw.* Our headlights found them — big and brown, round-headed and dark-eyed, sitting side by side in a dwarf cypress, Spanish moss brushing their feathers. We faced the car toward the show, shutting off the engine and keeping on the high beams. The owls hooted, then cater-wauled — raspy, unnerving sounds that cut through the Florida swamp. We called back, mimicking their resonant, doglike voices.

They answered. We answered. They answered each other. After five minutes of hoots, screams, and caterwauls, they floated across the road into a large pine. We started up again and ever so slowly returned down the broken road to Jerry's. When we arrived, no one was up.

A great horned owl serenaded us to sleep. In the morning Jerry told me a panther had passed through the campground three times during the past week, and two weeks ago, while he jogged east along the Loop Road, a big cat crossed in front of him, paused, then bounded into the brush. We missed the panther that day, but before we took down our tent an otter scooted across the front lawn, plunging into a lily pad pond behind Jerry's home. A big orange, black and white mangrove fox squirrel — a race of fox squirrel so rare that its entire range is confined to portions of four south Florida counties — climbed a wild tamarind tree in the front yard and began eating the broad fruit pods. Gallinules screamed. An osprey cried somewhere above us. I found a dead three-inch scorpion on the way to the showers and a handful of tapered land snail shells, each brightly colored with bands of blue, pink, yellow, and black. And we watched a pair of red-shouldered hawks consummate courtship on Jerry's TV antenna. Then we left, heading south for the Everglades and Flamingo.

We have been weaned so early in our lives from the mysteries of nature, that, unknowingly and sometimes willingly, we destroy our own natural heritage. No longer do we naturalists denounce the extinctions of plants and animals only; we mourn the loss of entire natural systems, whole watersheds and biologic communities. Vast stretches of nature unadulterated, wild as a Florida marl flat or a New England trout stream, are increasingly harder to find, and in our ignorance and prosperity we have let them pass, unnoticed.

The Kissimmee River, the birthplace of the Everglades, was a once-meandering hundred-mile-long river. It drained a chain of lakes whose northernmost member is not far from Disney World in central Florida, flowed through pond apple and willow swamps, meadows, marshes, and flat pine woodlands, and emptied into the northern end of Lake Okeechobee, a shallow 730-square-mile bowl of fresh water. In the late 1950s the Army Corps of Engineers converted the river into C-38, the straight-line Kissimmee Ditch. Prior to channelization, the Kissimmee entertained more than a million waterfowl each winter. In 1984 Johnny Jones, the executive director of the Florida Wildlife Federation, counted just eight ducks in the river on a winter's day. "That's eight," said Jones, "as in one, two, three, four, five, six, seven, eight!"

Before its development the slowly moving sheet of water that flowed through the Kissimmee into Lake Okeechobee and spilt into the Everglades triggered south Florida's rainy season. "The rain machine," it was called. Or as John Mitchell, writing for *Sierra*, called it, "the wild place that begins in the sky." South Florida may be part of the temperate zone, but the natural cycles there are tropical. There are two seasons, not four: the wet and the dry. Tremendous quantities of water ascend into the atmosphere by evaporation and transpiration each day from April to November. By midafternoon the buildup of atmospheric moisture is so great that rain heavily soaks the entire Kissimmee-Okeechobee-Everglades watershed. Life-giving rain.

After the Corps straightened the Kissimmee River, after Corps canals, levees, locks, and dams diverted water away from the Lake Okeechobee and the Everglades, the sheet flow stopped. Alligator Alley and the Tamiami Trail, which both cut the Glades east to west, blocked and bottlenecked the flow of rain water. Less water was exposed to evaporation. Less rain fell on south Florida, and life in the Fahkahatchee Strand State Preserve, Big Cypress National Preserve, and Everglades National Park had to share less and less water with a booming agricultural industry and a sprawling subtropical metropolis.

Towns all along both Florida coasts now siphon more and more water away from the Everglades. The Florida Keys grew at an alarming rate as well, and needing more water, piped it in from the Everglades. Condominiums and new retirement centers have sprung up. Corporate agriculture depletes rather than conserves valuable water, and lays bare miles of the Everglades with its rude industrial farming practices. Pesticides and chemical fertilizers wash into the Everglades. And the central Florida citrus industry, after suffering several years of frost damage and heavy financial losses, eyes the un-protected portions of the Everglades.

Fortunately, something is being done. Former Florida governor Bob Graham started the "Save Our Everglades Program," a multifaceted approach designed to restore the Kissimmee-Okeechobee-Everglades watershed by the turn of the twenty-first century. He authorized the purchase of 55,332 acres of world-class wildlife habitat in the eastern part of the Everglades, 110,000 acres in the western part of the Everglades, and 128,000 acres of Big Cypress Swamp. Graham also accepted and implemented a proposal by the National Park Service to allow a more natural flow of water into the western boundary of the park and agreed to an overall increase of water to a wider area of the park. The most encouraging project of the former governor's watershed restoration program is the gradual transfor-mation of C-38, the Kissimmee Ditch, to its former meandering, life-supporting ways. Eight miles of the ditch have already been reclaimed. On July 26, 1984, Bob Graham threw a shovelful of earth into the canal, marking the first time in the history of the United States that a state has take the initiative to undo a mistake made by the Army Corps of Engineers.

Nearly four thousand square miles of the watershed comprise the true Everglades, itself a river one hundred miles long and forty miles wide, with an average depth of six inches, where water creeps down a limestone plateau through sawgrass prairies and around tree islands called hammocks locally and eventually drains into Florida Bay. The Seminoles called it Pa-hay-Okee, the grassy waters. Marjory Stoneman Douglas, in her wonderful history of south Florida, called it *The Everglades: River of Grass*. From Lake Okeechobee to the bay, the land tilts fifteen feet, the riverbed sloping about three inches per mile. Water is the lifeblood of the region. Even familiar New England mammals — bobcat, black bear, white-tailed deer, cottontail — lead semi-aquatic lives here. Without it the glades dry up; alligators no longer bellow in the night, orchids stop blooming, and the wind sheds its bonnet of birds (since the mid-1800s, the population of long-legged wading birds in the Everglades has plummeted from 2.5 million to fewer than 250,000).

Before the first canals diverted water, the Everglades received the natural run-off of fifty to sixty inches of rain a year. Water meandered through a trackless, almost level sea of sawgrass (actually a sedge, *Claudium jamaicensis*) on its way to Florida Bay. During the August-to-November hurricane season, Lake Okeechobee overflowed its southern rim, watering the glades. Floodwater shimmering beneath the subtropical sun crawled inches a day, curving slightly toward the west, through the grassy river, tempering the six-month dry season by providing additional water after the rains stopped. In 1926 a hurricane flattened the sawgrass and spilled Okeechobee waters on the town of Moore Haven, killing three hundred people. Two years later another hurricane emptied the lake; eighteen hundred people drowned. Now dams and locks bottleneck the water, rupturing the natural sheet flow and sending either too much or too little down to the Everglades.

Everglades National Park, 2,020 square miles of wet, sun- drenched wilderness, occupies most of the southern tip of Florida and virtually all of Florida Bay, a shallow marl-bottomed bay that lies between the keys and the gulf and accepts the sheet flow that runs out of the Kissimmee-Okeechobee-Everglades watershed. Congress established the park in 1947, the first on Earth to be set aside for its abundant life forms rather than its spectacular geologic scenery. And in 1982 the United Nations designated the park a World Heritage Site, on a par with Tanzania's Serengeti plains and Ecuador's Galapagos Islands.

From Jerry's RV Campground we drove east toward Miami and then south into Homestead, "Gateway to the National Park." The ranger at the entrance booth told us she had recently seen a mother panther with three cubs cross the main park road two miles from her booth. For us, the panthers remained hidden. I did find a DOR pygmy rattlesnake, gray with black blotches and a broken brick-red line down its back, a DOR white-tailed deer attended by a cloud of vultures, and a DOR raccoon with fewer vultures in attendance.

Along the Anhinga Trail, a macadam path and a boardwalk along a portion of Taylor Slough, a shallow trough in the limestone that holds water all year and during the dry season teems with life, a great blue heron stood as still as stone on a shelf of limestone. It peered intently into the water, an inscrutable presence, big and gray, with a snakelike neck and a dagger bill. Behind the heron, willows put out fresh green leaves, ebony anhingas dried their wings, and a small alligator basked in the afternoon sun. A man standing next to me on the boardwalk announced that the heron had caught and eaten a boat-tailed grackle and a water snake the day before. Linny and I waited. An hour later the heron speared a catfish and tossed it onshore, beating and stabbing it with its long yellow bill. When the catfish stopped moving the heron picked it up crosswise in its bill, then flipped it in the air, recapturing it head first. With the catfish's spines laid back against its body, the heron began to swallow it. The fish bulged from the bird's neck like a rat going down a snake. Finished, the heron belched — *krahnuk!* — a bubble of sound that exploded from its mouth like air suddenly forced through a pipe.

We dined in twilight on the trail. Along the road to Flamingo, the only road through the park (a ride one clever park naturalist once called "thirty-eight miles of nothing") a sign read "Rock Reef Pass, Elevation 3 Feet." Small, light-colored moths rose from the sawgrass. Chuck-wills-widows and whip-poor-wills, hungry and silent, met the moths with gaping mouths, flitting back and forth in our headlights as they seined the night. Through the open sawgrass we found fresh DORs, mostly 'wills and one loggerhead shrike. Several were headless. Who had been scavenging? I wondered. Halfway to Flamingo we found out: a red-phased screech owl stood in the road picking the brains from a DOR whip-poor-will. As we stopped and watched, a bobcat crossed the road in our beams. Then a box turtle. Next a small brown marsh rabbit.

In Flamingo I stood at the southern tip of the Everglades, the southern tip of the continental United States, watching an almost half-moon traveling flat-side-up streak the thick gray water of Florida Bay. A breeze moved up from the southeast, over Cuba, across Key Largo, stirring the bay. The fronds of coconut palms clacked. A night heron squawked then squawked again, deep, gutteral sounds that amplified the night. Mullets chased by a predator fish peppered the surface of the bay. In the distance I heard bottle-nosed dolphins breathing, quick, sharp exhalations. Behind me a gallery of mangroves stretched inland along salty sloughs and tidal channels to form a dark wall, impenetrable and wild.

To the south verdant mangrove isles called keys — black smudges on the horizon — buffered the mainland against all but epic storms. Each of more than fifty keys is rooted in the shallow bay, and each is a bower of life. Oysters gather on the buttressed prop roots of red mangrove trees and strain the rich organic soup. Small fish are eaten by big fish, big, by bigger fish. We watched a silver tarpon jump and flash in the night.

After dark, when most people who stay over retreat to their campsites, the glades become wilder. I discovered that the laundromat at the Flamingo Lodge sponsored dull-green squirrel treefrogs, white-striped brilliant green treefrogs, and tiny hyperactive reef geckos that scurried around the walls and ceiling chasing insects. Raccoons were everywhere, raiding campsites, cars, and garbage pails. With our flashlights we caught the blue twinkling eye-shine of wolf spiders and the bright red eye-shine of hungry alligators that floated on the water's surface like logs. Spotting them Linny pursed her lips and sucked in air, making loud squeaking noises to invite their approach. Hearing her, the alligators slowly swam to our side of the shore, their eyes glowing in our flashlight beam.

Everywhere there was life, even in the men's room at the Long Pine Key Campground several miles south of the Anhinga Trail. As I waited one morning near the end of our trip in line at the sink, a big bronze treefrog with pop-eyes and huge suction-cup toes perched on a rafter: a Cuban treefrog, a five-and-a-half-inch goliath. I moved a green garbage pail under the rafter for support and climbed up. When I reached for the frog it moved. I reached again and it jumped. A short, squat man yelped below me. I climbed down and found the frog stuck to a mirror above the sink, inches from an unshaven ashen face. I apologized, removed the frog, and released it outside the bathroom.

Every morning at the walk-in campground in Flamingo we were visited by flocks of red-winged blackbirds and boat-tailed grackles that scavenged dried cereal and bread crumbs from our picnic table. Florida red-shouldered hawks, lighter and smaller and more trusting than those in Vermont, and black and turkey vultures came for hardier fare: bacon and chicken bones. One morning a turkey vulture ate an oil-soaked paper towel that I had used to drain bacon grease. Flocks of laughing gulls and black skimmers lined up in empty campsites. When the tide left Florida Bay, marbled godwits, short-billed dowitchers, and western sandpipers probed the marl flats in front of our tent. A great white heron, a large race of great blue heron, roosted in a buttonbush fifty feet from our tent. Its range is limited to the southern part of the park and the rock-hard Florida Keys, the old coral reefs that swing out for 120 miles from Key Largo to Key West. One afternoon a reddish egret lurched about with half-open wings in the shallow bay, picking at small fish.

Campers could stay at their campsite all day and watch the parade of birds move past, responding to the rhythm of the bay, or they could negotiate the backcountry. Deep in the mangroves along the Bear Lake Canoe Trail, kingfishers and little green herons moved ahead of our canoe. Small lines of roseate spoonbills, aloft and tropical as warm moist air, and arrows of white ibis pitched into the mangroves around a bend. Several alligators slid off mud banks. A shark, stranded by a storm tide in the shallow muddy water, thrashed forward as we approached. Dorsal and caudal fins cut the surface of the water. Its belly plowed the bottom as streams of mud spewed to the surface and drifted away in brown tendrils. The shark was trapped in the mangrove swamp; mud and gunk seeped into and clogged its spiracles as day by day breathing became more difficult in the oxygen-starved water. It was a fossil waiting to happen.

Beyond the struggling shark, a gray-brown crocodile with dark prominent cross bands relaxed on the bank. Slowly we paddled over. Its pointed head faced away from the water. When we got within ten feet of it, the crocodile sprang off the bank, turned completely around in midair, then dove under our canoe. A moment later it floated on the surface, watching us. At eight feet long, the crocodile was half grown, one of a dozen, I later learned, that had hatched near Bear Lake a decade before. Primarily a saltwater-dwelling fish-eater, its sunken eyes, pointy snout, and large, ostentatious teeth made the crocodile more sinister-looking than an alligator. With its eyes and forehead just above the surface of the water, the crocodile rose and sank as we paddled closer. He was perfectly at home in the rich estuarian mangrove swamp.

In 1870 American crocodiles patroled the Florida coast from Key West to Palm Beach on the Atlantic side and up the Gulf Coast to Charlotte Harbor. As few as two hundred American crocodiles — the northernmost race of a species whose range reaches south to Ecuador and Columbia, east to Cuba, and west along the Gulf Coast of Central America — survive today in the northeast corner of Florida Bay. Their days may be numbered. Only twenty active nests are known. Time-share condominiums, beach clubs, and recreational powerboats close in on Crocodile Lake National Wildlife Refuge on upper Key Largo.

After exploring the park by foot, boat, and car for more than a week, Linny and I decided to hire a pilot to fly us over the Everglades. A park naturalist recommended a tiny airstrip in the farm country east of the park. We drove over and found two crop dusters and a parachutists' jump plane in a short, crooked runway of mowed grass that ended in a wall of trees. The pilot who ran the shoestring operation greeted us. We struck a deal. The following morning at sunrise Linny and I went up in the jump plane.

With the jump door already off, nearly the entire side of the plane was opened to the elements. High-tension lines were strung above the road at the other end of the runway. I closed my eyes and held my breath as we cleared the wires. Once we were aloft, the glades spread below us in the first light of day, a tapestry of muted browns and greens and flashing water. Teardrop-shaped hammocks, where tropical hardwoods — gumbo limbo, mahogany, strangler fig, poison-wood — grew alongside red maples, live oaks, and other familiar temperate trees, punctuated the sawgrass islands in the tan prairie. From the air I saw the road to Flamingo that cut through the slash pine ridge only inches higher than the glades, through sawgrass prairies, and southward through the mangroves and coastal prairie, where hurricanes had dredged Florida Bay, piling miles of marl on the shoreline. Rock Reef looked like a long windbreak running north from the road into the sawgrass. A coterie of black vultures looked like gnats.

Birds were easier to spot. Royal terns and brown pelicans wheeled in the morning light, plunging headlong into the gray water. Egrets and herons lined up like dock pilings in the shallows, and behind one large mangrove key we spotted six hundred white pelicans. Squadrons of white ibis, varied flocks of shorebirds — mere specks from a thousand feet — settled on the gaping marl flats, facing the wind like fish schooled against the current. Six roseate spoonbills looking like glints of predawn light headed toward the mangroves for a day of feeding.

From the plane I saw the mixed communities merged into the whole vast wetland of south Florida: the pine ridge tapered into the sawgrass; a few hardy pines grew away from woods in the damp soil; the mangrove jungle ranged north from the bay, first as a wall then as isolated, dwarf trees that survived away from their normal saltwater habitat. High above the dense mangroves Linny and I saw flocks of spoonbills hemmed in by trees as they fed in tiny, hidden coffee-colored pools. It would have been impossible to reach them by canoe; they were many miles from the Bear Lake Trail through shallow, muddy water and tangled growth. From the air, even the natural channels in Florida Bay stood out. We wondered how we missed them one afternoon while canoeing, when we had gotten stranded on the marl flats as the tide went out.

Everything that man touched had hard angles. We could see it plainly from the air: the checkerboard farms that gave a touch of Kansas to the east side of south Florida, the migrant workers' dormitories, a state prison, and the condominiums. Water was bottlenecked along the north side of the Tamiami Trail and bulldozers pushed up everglades peat to make room for a new shopping center.

We landed for a few hours, then once again we went aloft, at sunset. We watched deer leave the hammocks. White ibis flew in long lines back from the bay and the mangroves to roost in the hammocks. From the side of the jump plane, I looked beyond the national park to the metropolitan haze of Miami and the southbound traffic streaming down U.S. Route 1. Bob Graham catalyzed the start of a restoration of the Kissimmee-Okeechobee-Everglades watershed. I found myself hoping his initative would gather force and roll back the advance of the developers. If wilderness is priceless, then Pa-hay-Okee, this river of grass, is in a class by itself. It exists nowhere else in the world. It belongs to the world.

15

WANTAGH REVISITED

THE MANDELBAUMS ARE GONE, retired to the east coast of Florida. Their bushes, larger and fuller, still command attention, but my old neighborhood has changed in other ways. Something more provocative than the color of houses and the size of woody vegetation is the urgent buzz of insects that fills the air. During a recent visit to friends on Long Island I found myself backtracking to my old neighborhood. I found a new microcosm developing among the European sycamores and Norway maples, the junipers and thorns there. And as usual, Mandelbaum's side of our property was at the forefront of the change.

I remember hearing cicadas when I was young. One or two males sang during the dog days, high in a hemlock behind our house. The sound was electronic, as though current escaped from the high voltage line above the backyard. The years have added cicadas to the neighborhood, thousands of them. Their song fills the suburban August days with a deafening buzz, the way peepers fill Vermont evenings in April. This audible transformation of Crest Road was awesome.

Of the three European sycamores my father had planted between the sidewalk and the road (he actually planted four, but one came down during a driving lesson), all buzzed with cicadas. The largest tree, the one next to Mandelbaum's, had fifty-nine split-open nymphal skins attached to the trunk and larger branches, and twenty-seven more on the ground close by. Each empty case — the remains of the last molt from which an adult cicada emerged — was a translucent brown, shiny as lacquer, an inch long and about a third as wide. All six legs ended in claws. The first pair, oversized and modified for digging, were spiked on the outside of the femur and looked like they belonged to a predatory insect, an ambush bug or a mantis, not a vegetarian. The remaining four legs fixed the case to the tree. Around the base of the sycamore were holes about half an inch wide where the nymphs had dug out of the soil. These were not red-eyed, black-and-orange-bodied periodical cicadas, the longest-lived insects in the world, but annual cicadas — green-eyed, black-bodied, dog-day harvestflies.

Unlike periodical cicadas, which live underground and suck root juices for seventeen years before emerging, each of these nymphs had lived underground for just three years. Although my field guide states that dog-day harvestflies disappear from mixed woods when the pines are cut, these cicadas fed on sycamore root sap. Only one pine graced the property, a thirty-foot white pine my father planted as a sapling in the early fifties. It grows on the far side of the driveway, an insurmountable distance for a nymph to burrow. The inch-long cicada nymphs rise close to their host tree on a couple of evenings in late August, climb up the trunk, a grass stem, or a dandelion leaf, and split open. An adult cicada emerges from the thorax of its nymphal case like a dragonfly or a butterfly.

I found a metamorphic adult. I plucked it from the sycamore, claws hooked to my finger, and watched it emerge. First its head, then its shoulders and wings were free. As the cicada leaned away from the old skin, gently rocking back and forth, her spiracles — white, nylonlike breathing tubes inside the nymphal skin — stretched to their limit and supported it like guy wires. When the cicada was half out, the spiracles snapped. A beautiful insect it was, soft and moist with bright green eyes and a turquoise tint to its pleated wings. Its thorax was cream white, its face brushed with gold, and as it pumped fluid through the veins of its wings, stretching them out, they took on a yellow cast. Its head, shaped like an isosceles triangle, supported two compound eyes on the far ends and a ventral mouth with a piercing and sucking tube at the apex. Between the compound eyes, three iridescent copper-colored simple· eyes — the ocelli — glowed like kaleidoscopic bits of light. In an hour its wings dried and its color changed. What was white became black. The turquoise shifted to green along the edge of the forewing, and black elsewhere. The yellow drained away.

Everywhere I walked I found the husks of dead cicadas. They littered the bases of trees, hung from the trunks, and peppered the sidewalk. Some were hollowed out where black ants had cut through the exoskeleton to feast on the bugs' soft innards. One cicada, still twitching, lay belly-up with a fly perched on its abdomen depositing eggs. Around the corner from the sycamore a flock of seven English sparrows convened in a crab apple, feeding on cicadas. A pair of blue jays feasted, too. Wherever the birds landed, cicadas flew from the tree and fanned out in all directions. I could hear them fly as they snapped their brittle, transparent wings, making a sound like so many giant bumblebees. Those that had succumbed to the lethargy that follows mating became easy pickings for the birds. A gray squirrel moved through a nearby Norway maple collecting cicadas, for the sheer number of these big insects rivaled the acorn output of the largest of the black oaks that still grew in the skinny greenbelt behind the synagogue. Even neighborhood cats ate the cicadas.

Beyond Mandelbaum's, in front of Skippy Packard's house, I watched a pair of cicadas mate on the sidewalk. They were back-to-back, like dogs in coitus, hooked together by the male's copulatory organ. When they were through the male slowly died as he always does after mating, while his mate flew to the closest tree. She climbed out on a twig and slit the bark with her ovipositor to lay her eggs. Four or five slits later, I left. She would cut more — maybe killing the twig in the process — depositing up to six hundred eggs, ten to twenty to a slit. When she finished, she would drop to the sidewalk or grass and die. Tiny nymphs would hatch in the twig, fall to the ground, then immediately burrow into the soil where they'd remain for three years, growing bigger with each of five instars, or molts. The only signs of the cicadas' departure would be dead twigs with cameos of brown leaves standing out against the wash of green.

Within three years, on a dark August night when the covetous eyes of birds are closed, the nymphs would emerge from the ground, climb the nearest tree, and undergo metamorphosis. During the two intervening summers other nymphs, larger and older, who have completed their subterranean engagement, would follow the ancient script and tunnel to the surface, making the song of the dog-day harvest-fly an annual event. With the song of the first male, other males would gather in the same tree and form a chorus. Their sound-producing organs, located below the base of the abdomen, are covered by two overlapping membranes which act like the heads of drums, amplifying the long, whining song. A primitive, seasonal orchestration would follow and move with the heat through suburban window screens.

One of the new kids, a ten-year-old girl whose inquiries into the natural world seemed limited or nonexistent (perhaps charred by television), zeroed in on me rather than on the rattling, singing trees alive with the cicadas' drone. Granted, it wasn't every day a man strolls down Crest Road with a clipboard and tape recorder in hand and a pair of binoculars around his neck. But the girl's world buzzed with a seasonal song that was as much a part of August as the sweat rolling off her forehead. I told her about cicadas, showed her the beautiful metamorphosing female, and gave her a handful of shed skins. "Yuck," she said, dropping them as though they were diseased.

In the early 1960s the roadside shack and the Wayside Bar and Grill were knocked down to make room for the Wantagh Oyster Bay Expressway, a six-lane highway that now connects the north and south shores of Long Island. Most of the vacant lot became the southbound on-ramp, and the remainder is periodically mowed by the county. No more orthopteran fiddlers. No more snakes. No more box turtles, lizards, or chipmunks. The toads were still in the

Jerusalem Avenue sump, but in reduced numbers. Filled with trepidation, I left Mandelbaum's and headed up Crest Road toward the remains of the vacant lot. Cicadas chorused all along the way. On the corner of Crest and Maxwell I found two items of interest: a pile of garbage and a dying Norway maple. I passed the garbage by and walked to the maple. The trunk was gray, weathered, and grim.

Three wasplike insects, fastened to the trunk by their ovipositors, stuck out at right angles as though pinned to the tree. They were stout, cylindrical, and dead. The membranous wings — long, thin and translucent — that lay back across their inch-long bodies looked varnished. Black and yellow-banded abdomens tapered to an ominous pointy horn. Stingers, I thought. I had never seen anything like them. Except for their broadly jointed thorax and abdomen (they lacked the pedicle or narrow waist of most hymenopterans), they looked like oversized wasps or hornets, maybe cicada killers.

While I stared in amazement, a living specimen flew over to the maple. Up and down the trunk it went, its short, beady antennae tapping the bark. Whenever it reached the ground, it turned abruptly and headed back up the tree. I placed a live cicada in its path. No interest. Well, maybe it wasn't hungry or maybe it wasn't a cicada killer. No interest either in its dead conspecifics. What was it doing? Why did it visit this dying maple but no healthy trees on Maxwell Drive? And where were they when I was growing up?

Just then a lanky black and yellow ichneumon wasp trailing a three-inch ovipositor, the largest I had ever seen, landed above the mystery insect. Her inch-long antennae vibrated up and down, twitching as she combed the bark like a dowser looking for water. When she found what she was after, the ichneumon arched up on all six legs, curled her abdomen under her body, and with her ovipositor looped back toward her head, inserted the threadlike organ into the wood, millimeter by millimeter. How something so long and thin could penetrate solid wood was beyond me.

Giant ichneumons, species *Megarhyssa*, are parasitoids, animals that lay their eggs on the eggs or larvae of a host species, in this case a host that inhabits dead or dying trees. Each *Megarhyssa* egg has a long filament at one end. As the egg passes down the ovipositor, the contents are squeezed into the filament. The slender egg resumes its normal spherical shape after it has reached the host. The ichneumon larva develops inside the host larvae, consuming it like a nightmare from the inside out. What was the ichneumon looking for? Certainly not cicadas, for their larvae hatch in twigs, not deep in the trunk. I wondered, too, if the strange-looking wasp and the ichneumon competed for the same host. The answers were not on the tree.

I drove to the Nassau County Natural History Museum, no longer called Tackapusha and no longer in an old white farmhouse, to explore their synoptic collection of Long Island insects and use their reference library. What I found was not what I had expected. The black-and-yellow banded wasplike insects were pigeon horntails, members of a primitive family of hymenopterans that lay their eggs in dead and dying wood. The female uses her ovipositor to bore through the trunk, then she deposits a single, slender egg in each bore hole. With each egg she places a cluster of fungal spores taken from a pocket in her abdomen. The sprouting fungus softens the wood, making it easy for the hatchling horntail larvae to tunnel and feed on the decaying wood. The larvae remain in the tree for two years, then spin cocoons of wood chips and silk, after which they pupate under the bark. After the last egg is set the female dies, often suspended on the tree trunk by her ovipositor. In wilder sections of the temperate deciduous forest woodland mice scavenge pinned horntail carcasses. Here in the suburbs, the carcasses stayed fixed to the tree, a grim but welcome sign of the recuperative powers of nature.

The big ichneumon, I discovered in the museum's library, had visited the Norway maple to parasitize the horntail larvae! Of the three species of *Megarhyssa* found in the eastern United States, all parasitize the pigeon horntail. Do they compete for the same horntail larva? As it turns out, they don't. Horntail larvae burrow to various depths in the wood, then follow the natural grain, tunneling around the tree. The three *Megarhyssa* species, which all have ovipositors of different lengths, specialize in larvae at a particular depth in the wood. The largest *Megarhyssa* has an ovipositor ten centimeters long, the smallest about four centimeters. Each female selects only those horntails at the maximum depth of her ovipositor, thereby reducing interspecific competition.

There is some dispute about how the *Megarhyssa* found the horntail larvae. It was clear to me from watching the wasp that her twitching antennae honed in on something. One reference said she presses her antennae against the bark to detect the vibration of the horntail larvae. Another claimed the ichneumon female locates her host by the presence of the symbiotic fungus that the female horntail injects into the wood. Since the horntail larvae feed on the fungus-softened wood, their frass (insect feces) is filled with fungus. The larger the larvae and the larger the frass, the easier it is for the searching ichneumon. Like a macabre science fiction character, a full-grown ichneumon larva chews through the horntail larvae, killing it. It pupates in the host's tunnel, and when metamorphosis is complete escapes through the bark.

I returned to the Norway maple the next day. There was no sign of the ichneumon wasp. The pigeon horntail was there, not far from where I left her pinned to the tree. I pulled her out, and with the aid of a magnifying lens examined her ovipositor. It was half drill, half hypodermic, stiff and beveled, and looked more like a weapon than a tool for penetrating wood. I placed the horntail in a vial, a memento — like the cicada cases — of the changing nature of my suburban roots.

Throughout most of the 1950s the greenbelt shrank as new ranch-style houses chipped into the woods, but it was severed, like the vacant lot, when the expressway came through. By the time I had my driver's licence the greenbelt was too small to satisfy my interest in nature. The sound of traffic drowned out the notes of the few remaining birds, and the wind had stopped humming in the trees. Today the woods are so thin that daylight is visible through them. It was hard to pretend the greenbelt was anything but a wilted tract, a remnant. Now there were more beer cans than birds. Briar tangles clogged forgotten trails; bricks and cinder littered the clearings.

The cottontails and opossums were gone, like the wolves and black bears of centuries before. I rolled over a log. A few millipedes, no salamanders. Although a resident had insisted a few snakes still lived behind the synagogue and still terrorized the neighborhood, I spent several hours looking for them, but found none. When I left the woods, a sign facing away from the dying greenbelt read, "This land will be sold at an auction by the County of Nassau." The greenbelt as I knew it had died, impaled on the sword of progress.

16

THE HEMLOCK'S TALE

As far as hemlocks go, it was no monster. I had examined much bigger trees, some more than four hundred years old with forty-inch diameters at breast height. A modest 131 years old, she had laid down her first growth ring in the fall of 1854 when Franklin Pierce, New Hampshire's only native son to ascend to the presidency, resided in The White House.

At 23½ inches in diameter at knee height, the hemlock was bigger than some of her neighbors, smaller than others. She stood on a knoll above the junction of Blood Brook and the Connecticut River in Norwich. From her trunk I could see across the river to Ledyard Bridge and the town of Hanover, from her crown I could have seen south to Mount Ascutney and north to the frosty shoulder of Mount Moosilauke. There was nothing unusual about the tree. It was just a good, healthy hemlock, part of a grove that added to the ambience of the recently purchased eighty-acre site for the Montshire's new museum and nature center. One Saturday afternoon in November 1985, she was felled.

Raw lumber was needed to build benches from which museum visitors could contemplate the scenery, and the hemlock, growing close to the trail and away from the trunks and larger branches of her neighbors, was rather unceremoniously singled out by the six-member trail crew. Three-fourths of the way through the trunk, the tree shuddered. Everyone but the cutter stepped aside as wood ripped and moaned and the crown tossed back and forth as though driven by wind. The tree's last few years of growth were not enough to keep her standing. When the hemlock fell, I stood there for a moment and pondered the tree, the stump, the pile of sawdust. As the rotating chainsaw blades dug through decades of rings, more than a century of hemlock history as well as the history of the Connecticut River Valley and the North Woods was laid bare.

Although hemlock seeds are winged, they don't travel far when they fall from the cone. I looked for the remains of a parent tree big enough and old enough to have sired this generation of hemlocks. There was no sign of one. It must have been dropped years ago, the bark no doubt sent to a tannery to cure leather, the naked trunk, slippery as the river's eels, sent downstream on a log drive to buffer the great columns of white pine on their long journey downstream. In the middle of the nineteenth century, hemlock wood, weak and splintery, had little other value.

In 1853, when the hemlock was still a seed sealed in its parent cone, Zadock Thompson, in his book *Natural History of Vermont*, declared that the wolverine was extinct in the state. With three-fourths of the state cleared for agriculture and sheep ranching, it is amazing that the wolverines lasted that long. White-tailed deer were gone by the 1850s according to Thompson, victims of unregulated hunting. Their absence was a blessing for all the young trees, for tender hemlock needles and twigs are the principal winter food of white-tailed deer in southern Vermont and New Hampshire.

In 1855, during the hemlock's second year of growth, mowing machines appeared in New Hampshire, and three years later the wooden plough was replaced by the cast iron plow. It made land-clearing and stump-removal easier. But by then the handwriting was on the barn: farmers abandoned the stony soil of northern New

England for the soft prairie sod of Ohio, Indiana, Illinois, and Iowa. Idle farms and pastures slowly filled with red and white pine and gray birch.

In 1860, when the hemlock was a spindly six-year-old sapling, 42 percent of all native-born Vermonters lived outside their state, leaving cellar holes and stonewalls as vestiges of their passing. The lilacs and apple trees that had bloomed in their dooryards now decorated the second coming of the northern hardwood forest. The young hemlock, perched on a knoll that once hosted sheep, laid down a lot of wood those first few years, enough to get a jump on her siblings.

In 1864 George Perkins Marsh — a lawyer, scientist, linguist, philosopher, naturalist, and staunch product of Vermont — wrote *Man and Nature*, the first attempt at formulating a conservation ethic in the United States. From his home in Woodstock, six miles down the Connecticut River and thirteen miles east of the hemlock, Marsh called for the management of renewable resources — timber, wildlife, and soil — and for the evaluation of man's role in the grand scheme of nature. Few listened then.

New railroads crisscrossed both states, running up and down and across the Connecticut River, and kept abreast of the growing forest. Each engine burned one thousand cords of wood a year; in addition, tens of thousands of wooden ties were needed for the roadbeds. Nobody bothered the hemlock in 1865. At less than two inches in diameter she was useless save only to songbirds, small animals, the knoll, and the river.

In 1866 a freak tornado swirled across the Connecticut, toppled a toll bridge upstream in Barnet, Vermont, and sent its splinters past the hemlock. A year later the last parcel of state-owned land in New Hampshire — a 172,000-acre tract that included Mount Washington, the highest mountain north of the Smokies and east of the Black Hills — was sold for $25,000, about $6.88 an acre.

By 1870 Grafton County, New Hampshire, had 442,738 acres cleared for farming, about 40 percent of its total acreage. Bluebirds and purple martins were abundant, nighthawks rode the twilight everywhere, and farm boys hunted cottontails. Dogs ravaged Vermont sheep throughout most of the 1870s until farmers were forced to butcher their own flocks to reduce their losses. No coyotes to blame then. When Custer sank the seventh calvary in 1876, the hemlock was twenty-two years old and a little more than two inches in diameter.

Luckily for the hemlock, white-tailed deer were still so scarce that Vermont imported seventeen from New York in 1878 to bolster its dwindling herd. The hemlock had other problems, though. The early 1880s marked a period of slow growth. Her rings, bunched very close together, showed that the knoll was carpeted with saplings, each struggling for a limited amount of water, nutrients and sunlight.

On Thanksgiving Day, 1881, Alexander Crowell shot the last known mountain lion in Vermont. The hemlock and the rest of the Green Mountain state had no reason to give thanks.

In 1885 the last passenger pigeons in New Hampshire were shot, eliminating what had once been called "a divine gift of protein." No longer did wild flocks arrow up the Connecticut Valley, blot out the sun, or stop to cavort in the hemlock's crown. Ten years later New Hampshire, never a state to miss a chance to enact landmark environmental legislation, closed the hunting season and granted the pigeons complete protection.

On February 5, 1887, a train wreck in White River Junction killed thirty people, and three months later a fire gutted the mill area of Lebanon, destroying eighty buildings and leaving six hundred people jobless. For the hemlock, another ring.

When the Great Blizzard of 1888 swept through the Connecticut Valley, the hemlock weathered the storm. Other trees were less fortunate. Later that year the New Hampshire State Department of Agriculture proclaimed man's avarice for lumber had outstripped the forest's ability to regenerate itself; the annual wood harvest had reached twice the reproductive rate. With the disappearance of old-growth woods went the land's ability to hold water. Mountain springs, once hidden by arches of spruce and hemlock, faced the sun and dried up, and trout streams that had flowed all year became seasonal.

In 1890 Austin Corbin, a wealthy New York businessman, bought and fenced twenty-five thousand acres of rugged hill and pasture land that extended into Croydon, Newport, and Cornish, thirty miles southeast of the hemlock. Corbin released deer, moose, elk, caribou, European wild boar, and bison on his preserve. Later the bison herd became a source for captive-breeding at the Bronx Zoo; the zoo's program then served to restock western parks. The rest of the animals roamed unmolested, but open to public viewing until Corbin's death. New management then shut out the public and converted the park to an exclusive hunting preserve.

In 1892 Rudyard Kipling, living in Brattleboro sixty miles downriver from the hemlock, began his two-volume *Jungle Book* which accomplished as much for snakes as did the Book of Genesis. To the west, near the plains of the Ottauquechee River, the Woodstock Inn opened that same year, the first step in the conversion of a sleepy dairy town into a playground for the wealthy.

In 1894, after sixty-two years in the U.S. Pharmacopeia, pitch from eastern hemlocks was no longer recognized as a counter irritant for chronic rheumatic pains. The hemlock slipped from her medicinal pedestal, but a place in history was still assured it. Canada credits the tree with having saved the first European explorers from scurvy. A tea of steeped needles and twigs, rich in vitamin C and tasting like warm turpentine, helped keep the wheels of progress turning by saving the settlers, but sealed the fate of the Iroquois who brewed and shared the drink.

By 1900 woodland caribou, never more than casual visitors to New Hampshire and Vermont, were seen for the last time in either state as a herd of seventeen milled about the First Connecticut Lake, headwaters of the Connecticut River. In 1901 the Society for the Protection of New Hampshire's Forests was born the same year Teddy Roosevelt became the 26th president of the United States. Roosevelt began the national forest system, and the society lobbied for the creation of the White Mountain National Forest. Without its efforts to promote the wise use of natural resources, the mantle of hardwood and conifer that stretches across ancient granite hills, gripping the soil and shading trout streams, would have followed the path of New Hampshire's last wolves (which were all shot by 1895). On grew the hemlock, unaware that the foundation of modern conservation had just been laid.

In 1902 Vermont lost its last wolf.

In 1903 a fire consumed two hundred thousand acres of New Hampshire forest. Two years later state legislators failed to pass an adequate fire-protection bill. They did try to help the beaver, however. In 1905 New Hampshire granted the beaver complete protection forty-seven years after the animals had disappeared from the state.

Concerned about destructive logging operations throughout the Appalachian Mountains, Congress passed the Weeks Act in 1911 and appropriated $11 million to buy privately owned land in North Carolina and New Hampshire. This was the seed money for the White Mountain National Forest, the first national forest in the East.

January 7, 1911 marked the beginning of the Meridan Bird Club, the first to own and maintain a bird sanctuary. To commemorate the event two years later, Eleanor and Margaret Wilson, Woodrow Wilson's daughters, dressed up as birds and fluttered about on stage during the premier of Percy MacKay's masque, *Sanctuary*, on Augustus Saint-Gaudens estate in Plainfield, New Hampshire. Among the luminaries in attendance were President Wilson and Plainfield, New Hampshire resident Maxfield Parish. The hemlock, anchored to her knoll, missed the show.

In 1915 the hemlock reached 4½ inches in diameter, not yet a strapping tree but tall enough to raise her pyramidal crown above her neighbors in full view of the largest log drive in the history of the Connecticut River. Two men died, pinched between white pine trunks, as sixty-five million feet of lumber, mostly mammoth white pine taken from the headwaters of the Connecticut and a few debarked hemlocks, tore great chunks from the river's banks.

The log drive, the last on the Connecticut, was a success; the International Paper Company and the Connecticut Valley Lumber Company had wrung the last dollar out of the New Hampshire hills just before the dedication of the White Mountain National Forest was to take place later that year. Also in 1915, a pair of starlings nested in Hanover and an opossum was trapped in Warner, New Hampshire, forty miles southeast of the hemlock; the first was a town record, the second a state record.

In 1916 the Old Man of the Mountain, immortalized by Nathaniel Hawthorn and chosen as the New Hampshire state symbol, was judged in need of a face lift. Edward H. Geddes stabilized the hallowed profile with turnbuckles. Turnbuckles weren't used to help the hemlock when her perch began to erode, so she added more wood to her south side, breaking the symmetry of her rings.

In 1918 the United States Migratory Bird Treaty Act became law, setting seasons and bag limits on waterfowl, shorebirds, and seabirds on the brink of extinction. A year later the White Mountain National Forest grew to 430,000 acres.

The 1920s marked the end of seven decades of slow growth for the hemlock. It marked other events, too. In 1920 Virgil White stripped a Model T Ford, replaced the front wheels with five-foot runners, and added a traction belt over the rear wheels. Two years later White built seven Model T snowmobiles. Between 1924 and 1928 his factory produced twenty-five thousand machines. Winter hasn't been the same ever since. Neither were the Boston Red Sox after they sold Babe Ruth to the Yankees in 1920. Fortunately for the hemlock, white ash made a better bat.

In 1922 two wolverine cubs were taken from a Coos County den, the last wolverines recorded east of Minnesota. At about the same time, a pair of mountain lions roamed the east side of the Androscoggin River from the south shore of Lake Umbagog to Cambridge. Since then rumors have replaced them in New Hampshire.

In 1929 Vermont closed the fisher season; New Hampshire followed suit in 1934.

In 1930 Vermont had more cows than people, made more butter than cheese, and was working with the deeded estate of Marshall J. Hapgood, which would mark the beginning of the Green Mountain National Forest. A year later a trail extended from Sherburne Pass in the Green Mountains to Woodstock, making it possible to ski or hike from Hanover to Vermont's Long Trail. Both sections were incorporated into the Appalachian Trail System in 1926. The trail reached Ledyard Bridge from the north side of Blood Brook, so for the last fifty-nine years of her life the hemlock looked over the Georgia-to-Maine hikers. They probably never noticed; she was just another tree in a long wave of second-growth forest.

On April 25, 1932, Herbert Clark Hoover, the thirty-first president of the United States, signed a proclamation making the Green Mountain National Forest the second national forest in the Northeast.

The thermometer plunged to fifty below in Bloomfield, Vermont, on December 30, 1933, the coldest temperature ever recorded in New England. The hemlock weathered the cold but lesser trees popped and snapped like firecrackers. The following year, a 231-mile-per-hour wind, the strongest gust ever recorded in the world, raked the top of Mount Washington, and the world's first rope tow was put in operation on the Suicide Six trail in Woodstock. The first event made a mountain famous, the second sealed the fates of hundreds of others.

Gray squirrels marched across the covered bridge between Cornish and Windsor in 1935, and kept marching west for nearly two years.

By 1937 the White Mountain National Forest had grown to 700,000 acres, making the federal government the largest landowner in New Hampshire. That year New England trees produced a bumper crop of seeds.

The following year, on September 25, 1938, the Great Hurricane roared up the Connecticut River, toppling millions of trees (there was enough downed timber to build 200,000 five-room homes) and killing six hundred people. It was the worst storm in New England's history. For the hemlock, another ring.

In 1941 Vermont repealed its bounty on black bear.

1944 was just another year for the hemlock, but for northern New England it marked the arrival of the eastern coyote. Again, the hills and river valleys filled with wondrous canticles.

Between 1945 and 1955 the hemlock prospered, laying down more wood than at any other period. Her one and a half inches of growth were a sign of the times. World War II had ended and the Baby Boom had begun. America was faultless. But beyond the hemlock the lazy Connecticut, thick and brown with the offal of civilization, told a different story. The river was ill. Pulp waste from paper mills and raw sewage poisoned it. There was no swimming or fishing allowed, and the wooded banks, free from development because no one could stand the smell of the river, were a graveyard for rusted automobiles. Only bacteria thrived in the Connecticut River, dining on bloated cows and sundry other organic wastes.

In 1946 the Soil Conservation Service started a farm-improvement program for Vermont and New Hampshire farmers. There were thirty-three steps to follow, several of which benefited wildlife. The Montshire Museum crew followed one when we cut down the hemlock, building brush-pile shelter belts for wildlife. White-footed mice and tree sparrows came to the dense needles and reddish bark ground cover.

A pair of bald eagles fledged two young above the northwest corner of Lake Umbagog in 1949. The tree still stands, but eagles never again nested in the state.

Wilder Dam turned back the Connecticut in 1950, and with it went the shoreline north to Bradford. Below the dam the water level rose and fell at human whim, stranding bank beaver and muskrat and softening the contours of Sumner's Falls, the last stretch of white water on the river.

In 1953, when the hemlock was ninety-nine years old, a lynx wandered into Grafton County, New Hampshire, paused in a stand of red spruce, and was shot. The state had posted a twenty-dollar bounty for the last gray bobtailed cat of the Upper Valley, and the hills lost a confidant.

After 1954 Vermont's peregrine falcons, like New Hampshire's bald eagles, succumbed to DDT. Their inaccessible aeries, tucked in ledges high above rivers and lakes, stained white by generations of use, fell silent. The following year the New Hampshire Fish and Game Department created the Wilder Refuge, roughly two and a half miles of Connecticut River shoreline in Lyme consisting of two fifty-acre inlets and twenty acres of sloughs and potholes. The refuge, a by-product of water impounded by Wilder Dam, offered sanctuary to wood ducks and black ducks, except during the hunting season.

After 1955 the hemlock's growth slowed, but the Upper Valley began to boom. In 1968 Interstate 89 crossed the Connecticut River from New Hampshire, reaching Sharon, Vermont. Three years later

Interstate 91 reached Fairlee, Vermont. No event since the Ice Age had caused as much change. People came by the thousands, and thousands more are still coming. The hemlock, unperturbed, grew through it all, her branches sweeping out from her trunk, her small, dark green needles absorbing the filtered sunlight. How was she to know that the highways would bring the people that would create the museum that would buy the land upon which she grew, and render her into benches.

Farms were sold — some were virtually stolen. The strip of riverine land in West Lebanon that once hosted corn fields and a mature flood plain forest of elm, black willow, bitternut hickory, and red and silver maple lost all integrity, becoming an Anywhere USA. Gone was the last unblemished stand of old-growth riparian woods along the upper Connecticut River. In its place now is a sewage treatment plant, a Grand Union, a K-Mart.

And gone, too, by the early 1970s were most of New Hampshire's fishers; 1,130 were trapped — more than 200 by one greedy man in 1971 — another 1,008 the following year. As long as the legislature controlled the season, the fisher were doomed. At the same time, Vermont's fishers came back. Between 1957 and 1969 Vermont released 124 Maine fishers in forty-one townships, and by 1971 the big mustelids had reclaimed most of their former stomping grounds in the state. Vermont then brought back the wild turkey, releasing 41 Pennsylvania birds in 1969. As if to make amends, New Hampshire lawmakers removed the lynx bounty in 1973, but the fisher season was still three months long on the east side of the river.

The hemlock lived long enough for the 1972 Clean Water Act to produce one of the greatest environmental turnarounds of the century. No longer do the Connecticut's pickerel and walleye float downstream belly-up, and no longer do canoes come ashore stained with sludge.

On January 10, 1976, the Montshire Museum opened its doors to the public. Eight years later the land on which the hemlock stood changed hands. The Hanover Cooperative Society sold seventy-five acres of Norwich, Vermont, river-front property to the Montshire Museum for its new building site.

Nine species of hemlock fringe the moist temperate zones of the northern hemisphere. Four grow in North America, two in the West and two in the East — the Carolina and the eastern hemlocks. Our tree, whose wood now offers a respite for hikers along the Montshire Museum's trail system, is one of the principal trees of the northern hardwood forest, and together with sugar maple, yellow birch, and American beech forms the climax stage of forest succession throughout most of northern New England. To a botanist she was *Tsuga canadensis*; to siskins and purple finches, a source of seeds. For deer, she held back the snow and filled their bellies. For me, she was a forest matriarch, the quintessential winter conifer, the essence of every Christmas card. We carried her three benches one at a time, three men to each side like pallbearers.

The hemlock had laid down her last ring in 1985. For 131 years she had hugged the knoll as the convoluted land around her changed from bucolic farms to second-growth woods, dense and dark. Fishers and snowshoe hare returned, ravens and goshawks. Even moose. Before her the great predators disappeared, the lion, the wolf, the lynx. Developments sprout in the valley like fields of ragweed and bur. It is progressively harder to find solitude in the gnarled hills, as the whine of snowmobiles, all-terrian vehicles, and motorbikes invade the remote corners of those precious places. At stake is the very soul of the North Country.

I know this. I grew up in suburbia and watched my greenbelt shrivel, my vacant lot come undone. I came here, to the Upper Valley, myself half Levittown, half wilderness, a part of the problem but also, I hope, a part of the solution.

ACKNOWLEDGMENTS

I OWE MANY THANKS to my friends at the Montshire Museum of Science, particularly to Joan Waltermire, whose illustrations grace this book, for her generous support and encouragement, and to Director David Goudy for continuing the late Bob Chaffee's dream. To my former editors at the *Valley News*, Russell Powell and Steve Gordon, I am grateful for their interest in natural history. To my current editor, Dan Mackie, who gracefully accepted missed deadlines and thin columns during the past four months as I finished the final draft of *Backtracking*, I owe both my gratitude and my apologies.

I owe thanks to my publishers at Chelsea Green, Ian and Margo Baldwin, for their commitment to quality and for their patience during the two years it took this book to evolve. Every piece of writing needs a good editor. I am indebted to Ian for his gentle suggestions and sensitive eye and ear, and to Wanda Shipman for her surgically precise copyediting. Many friends helped me by gathering facts, answering questions, or reading portions of earlier versions of my manuscript. Thank you: William Ballard, Professor Emeritus of Biology, Dartmouth College; Peter Stettenheim, former editor of *The Condor*; and John Hay, Richard Miller, Sandra Miller, Bev

ACKNOWLEDGMENTS

Petellin, Ted and Patty Armstrong, Joey Lopisi, and Diane Haas. Thanks also to David Brooks and Leslie Wilfong, and to Steven and Josie Rashkin, who were gracious hosts to a hungry, itinerant naturalist.

Thanks to my parents for accepting a naturalist when they had hoped for a surgeon, and for tolerating all of the creatures I brought home.

And to Linny I owe my deepest appreciation. You listened to and read every word of every draft. Several times. Without your love, encouragement, and devotion to this project, there would have been no book at all.

BACKTRACKING: THE WAY OF A NATURALIST was designed by Dede Cummings. It was typeset in Garamond Antiqua by Whitman Press. It was printed on Warren's Sebago, an acid-free paper, by Halliday Lithograph.